The Making of English

THE
Making of English

By Henry Bradley

M.A., HON. D.LITT., OXON.; HON. LITT.D., DURHAM
HON. D.LITT., SHEFFIELD; PH.D., HEIDELBERG
FELLOW OF MAGDALEN COLLEGE, OXFORD
FELLOW OF THE BRITISH ACADEMY

With an Introduction by Bergen Evans

and additional material and notes by Professors
Bergen Evans and Simeon Potter

WALKER AND COMPANY

NEW YORK · LONDON

Library of Congress Catalog Card Number: LC 67-23651

First published in the United States of America
in 1967 by Walker and Company, a division of
Publications Development Corporation.

PRINTED IN THE UNITED STATES OF AMERICA

Introduction by Bergen Evans

Written at the turn of the century, *The Making of English* still serves its avowed purpose: "to give to educated readers unversed in philology some notion of the causes that have produced the excellences and defects of modern English." And were it to be rewritten, few changes if any would have to be made. Nowhere near so many, for instance, as have had to be made in the revised versions of Fowler's *Modern English Usage* or Strunk's *The Elements of Style*.

Rarely have learning and lucidity been so happily combined. Beginning with a deceptively simple statement of the likenesses of German and English, Bradley moves on to their dissimilarities and, almost before we know it, he has sketched out for us the character of Anglo-Saxon. From there on, his purpose, as he states, is not to treat of the changes that have taken place in chronological sequence but "to give some idea of the causes by which the more remarkable changes were brought about, and to estimate the effect which these changes have had" on the fitness of English as an instrument for the expression of thought.

Interspersed with all of this are stimulating insights into the nature of language. His discussion, for instance, of the symbolism of certain sounds (pp. 110-112) and why this gives some words "a natural fitness" is stirring and challenging. And such passages as his analysis of the hidden forces that give *preposterous* and *emergency* their effectiveness (pp. 144-145), though they fill only a few lines, should start many a student on a course of creative wondering.

Here and there, to be sure, the reader is startled by something that dates the book—*to maffick* (p. 102), for

[v]

example, or the passing reference to "the *key* with which we wind up a watch." But the mild shock of coming on these few anachronisms is eloquent testimony to the remarkably contemporary nature and tone of the whole.

Bradley has his crotchets, but they are advanced with extraordinary mildness—particularly when one considers the irascibility and dogmatism with which most grammatical pronouncements are trumpeted forth. His footnote (p. 50) on the "correct" use of *do* as an auxiliary simply doesn't represent contemporary usage and, apparently, did not in his own day, since he confesses ruefully that "many American writers" ignored the fine distinction he had delineated and that a laxness in regard to it "appears to be gaining ground in England" as well.

In a like manner he allows his longing to get a little ahead of his learning when he states that the distinction between *shall* and *will,* as auxiliaries, had, after centuries of groping, finally been established. And even then his honesty forces him to confess (pp. 47-52) that "Scotchmen and Irishmen still find it difficult to master."

But these are trifles, rare glimpses of the Victorian gentleman underneath the scholar. For the greater part, the scholar is firmly in control and the gentleman merely sees to it that he graceful and good-natured. The work is as sound as it is simple.

BERGEN EVANS
Northwestern University

PUBLISHER'S NOTE: The present edition of *The Making of English* follows the original edition in all respects. The reader will notice that Bradley is occasionally inconsistent in the spelling of certain words and names. Shakespeare, for example, appears variously as "Shakspere," "Shakespere" and "Shakespeare." Everyday is given both as "everyday" and, more frequently, "every-day."

Asteriks indicate footnote amplifications and comments by Simeon Potter, all of which are identified as such.

Author's Preface

This little work was announced as in preparation some years ago, but illness compelled me to lay it aside when only a few pages had been written, and since then my health has seldom permitted me to attempt any work in addition to my daily task as one of the editors of the *Oxford English Dictionary*. Some of the faults of this volume may be due to the desultory manner in which it has been composed; but, on the other hand, the length of time that has elapsed since it was first planned has given me opportunity for more careful consideration of difficult points.

The object of the book is to give to educated readers unversed in philology some notion of the causes that have produced the excellences and defects of modern English as an instrument of expression. With the history of the language I have attempted to deal only so far as it bears on this special problem. The subject, even as thus restricted, is one which it is not easy to treat briefly. I have, however, resisted the temptation to enlarge the volume beyond the limits originally intended, because I believe that for the purpose which I have in view a small book is more likely to be useful than a large one.

My thanks are due to my friends Professor Napier, Mr. W. A. Craigie, and Mr. C. T. Onions, for their kindness in reading the proofs, and suggesting valuable corrections and improvements.

HENRY BRADLEY
Oxford, January, 1904

Contents

I

Introductory

1. THE LIKENESS OF GERMAN AND ENGLISH.

An Englishman who begins to learn German cannot fail to be struck by the resemblance which that language presents to his native tongue. Of the words which occur in his first lessons because they are those most commonly used in everyday conversation, a very large proportion are recognisably identical, in spite of considerable differences of pronunciation, with their English synonyms. The following examples will suffice to illustrate the remarkable degree of similarity between the vocabularies of the two languages: *Vater* father, *Mutter* mother, *Bruder* brother, *Schwester* sister, *Haus* house, *Feld* field, *Gras* grass, *Korn* corn, *Land* land, *Stein* stone, *Kuh* cow, *Kalb* calf, *Ochse* ox, *singen* to sing, *hören* to hear, *haben* to have, *gehen* to go, *brechen* to break, *bringen* to bring, *gut* good, *wohl* well, *grün* green, *hart* hard, *blind* blind, *ich* I, *wir* we, *selbst* self, *hier* here, *unter* under, *bei* by, *vor* be-fore. At a very early stage of his progress, the learner will find himself able to compile a list of some hundreds of German words which have an obvious likeness to the English words with which they agree in meaning.

In addition to these resemblances which lie on the sur-

face, there are many others which can only be perceived
by the help of a knowledge of the general laws of correspondence between German and English sounds. A few of
these general laws may be mentioned by way of illustration.
An English *t* is usually represented in German by *z, tz,* or
ss; an English *th* by *d;* an English *p* by *pf* or *f;* an English
d by *t;* and an English *v* in the middle of a word by *b.*
There are similar laws, too complicated to be stated here,
relating to the correspondence of the vowels. By the study
of these laws, and of the facts that are known about the
history of the two languages, scholars have been enabled
to prove the fundamental identity of a vast number of
English words with German words which are very different
from them in sound and spelling, and often in meaning.
Thus, for example, *Baum,* a tree, is the same word as the
English 'beam'; *Zaun,* a hedge, is our 'town' (which originally meant a place surrounded by a hedge, a farm enclosure); *Zeit,* time, is our 'tide'; *drehen,* to turn, wind, is our
'throw,' and the derivative *Draht,* wire, is our 'thread';
tragen, to carry, is our 'draw'; and so on.

But it is not merely in their stock of words that English
and German have a great deal in common. In their grammar, also, they resemble each other to a very remarkable
extent. Our way of forming the genitive by adding *s* is
paralleled in many German words: 'the king's house' is in
German 'des Königs Haus.' The syllables *-er* and *-est* are
used in both languages to form the comparatives and super-
latives of adjectives. In the conjugation of the verbs the
similarity is equally striking. 'I hear,' 'I heard,' 'I have
heard' are in German *ich höre, ich hörte, ich habe gehört;*
'I see,' 'I saw,' 'I have seen' are *ich sehe, ich sah, ich habe
gesehen;* 'I sing,' 'I sang,' 'I have sung' are *ich singe, ich
sang, ich habe gesungen;* 'I bring,' 'I brought,' 'I have

brought' are *ich bringe, ich brachte, ich habe gebracht.*
Our 'thou singest' is in German *du singst.*

The explanation of these facts is not that English is
derived from German or German from English, but that
both have descended, with gradual divergent changes, from
a prehistoric language which scholars have called Primitive Germanic or Primitive Teutonic. Low German or
Plattdeutsch, the dialect spoken (now only by the common
people) in 'Low' or Northern Germany, is much more like
English than literary High German is; and Dutch and
Frisian resemble Low German. The Scandinavian languages, Swedish, Danish, Norwegian, and Icelandic, are
also of Germanic (or Teutonic) origin; and so is Gothic,
a dead language known to us chiefly from a translation of
portions of the Bible made in the fourth century.

2. DIFFERENCES BETWEEN GERMAN AND ENGLISH.

But while modern English and modern German have
so many conspicuous traces of their original kinship, the
points of contrast between the two languages are equally
striking and significant.

In the first place, the grammar, or rather the accidence,
of German is enormously more complicated than that of
English. The German noun has three genders, which in
many instances have no relation to the sex of the object
signified, or to the meaning or form of the word. *Kopf,*
head, is masculine, though the synonymous *Haupt* is neuter; *Hand* is feminine, but *Fusz,* foot, is masculine, and
Bein, leg, is neuter; *Weib,* woman, and *Mädchen,* girl,
are neuter. The foreign student of English has no such
difficulties to encounter. Properly speaking, we have no

'genders' at all: we say 'he,' 'she,' or 'it' according to the sex, or absence of sex, of the object to which we refer. English nouns have only one case-ending, the *s* of the genitive; and practically only one mode of forming the plural, as the few exceptions can be learned in half-an-hour. German nouns have four cases, and are divided into several declensions each with its own set of inflexions for case and number. The English adjective is not inflected at all; the one form *good* corresponds to the six German forms *gut, guter, gute, gutes, gutem, guten,* the choice of which depends partly on the gender, number, and case of the noun which is qualified, and partly on other grammatical relations. In conjugating an English verb, such as *sing,* we meet with only eight distinct forms, *sing, singest, sings, singeth, sang, sangest, singing, sung;* and even of these, three are practically obsolete. In the conjugation of the German verb *singen* the number of distinct forms is sixteen.

In addition to these differences in the grammatical systems of the two languages, there are others no less noteworthy which relate to the character of their vocabulary.

We have already pointed out that of the English words which occur in familiar conversation, the great majority are found to exist also in German, with certain regular variations of form due to the difference in the sound-systems of the two languages. If, however, instead of confining our attention to that part of the language that serves the needs of everyday life, we were to examine the whole English vocabulary as it is exhibited in a dictionary, we should find that by far the greater number of the words have no formal equivalents in German, being for the most part derived from foreign languages, chiefly French, Latin, and Greek. It is true that many of these non-Germanic words are very rarely used; still, if we take at random a page from an English book which treats of history, politics, philosophy, or literary criticism, the majority of the nouns, adjectives, and verbs are usually of foreign etymology. An ordinary page of German, on the other hand, contains very few words that are not derived from native roots. German, in fact, is, comparatively speaking, an unmixed language; modern English, so far as its vocabulary is concerned, is a mixed language, in which the native Germanic elements are outnumbered by those derived from foreign tongues.

3. CHARACTERISTICS OF OLD ENGLISH.

The differences between German and English, *so far as they have been described above,*[1] are entirely due to the gradual changes that have taken place in English during the last thousand years. The ancient form of our language —the kind of English that was written by King Alfred in the ninth century—had every one of those general characteristics which we have mentioned as distinguishing modern German from modern English.

Before proceeding to the illustration of this statement, let us briefly explain the meaning of certain terms which we shall have to use. By 'Old English' we mean the language (by some persons called 'Anglo-Saxon') spoken by Englishmen down to about 1150; 'Middle English' is the language spoken between about 1150 and about 1500;

[1] This limitation is very important. It must not be imagined that German has not altered greatly during the last thousand years, or that English and German did not already differ widely from each other a thousand years ago.

and 'Modern English' means the English of the last four centuries. The reader must not, however, suppose, as young learners sometimes do, that in 1150 or in 1500 one kind of English was superseded by another. The English language has been undergoing constant change ever since it was a language, and it is changing still. For purposes of study it has been found useful to divide its history into three periods; and if this is done at all, it is necessary to specify some approximate dates as the points of division. The dates 1150 and 1500 have been chosen because the one is the middle and the other the end of a century of the common reckoning; and they are also convenient, because about those years the process of change was going on somewhat more rapidly than usual, so that if we compare a book written a quarter of a century before the end of a period with one written a quarter of a century after it, we can see clearly that the language has entered on a new stage of development.

In considering the characteristics of Old English, we will refer especially to the southern dialect as it was written by King Alfred just before 900. In the first place, Alfred's English had all the grammatical complexity which exists in modern German, and indeed a little more. It had the same irrational system of genders: *hand* was feminine, *fōt* (foot) was masculine, while *mægden* (maiden) and *wīf* (wife, woman) were neuter. The Old English nouns had five cases, and the system of declensions was intricate to a degree which modern German does not nearly rival. Some nouns made their genitive singular in *-es*, others in *-e*, others in *-a*, and others in *-an*; and in a few nouns the genitive had the same form as the nominative. The endings which marked the nominative plural were *-as, -a, -u, -e, -an*; moreover, many plural nominatives coincided in form with the singular, and others were formed (like our modern *teeth* and *mice*) by change of vowel. The adjectives had an elaborate set of inflexions, which have now utterly disappeared, so that the solitary Modern English form *glad* represents eleven distinct forms in Old English: *glæd, glædre, glædne, glædra, gladu, glades, gladum, glade, gladena, glada, gladan*. In the conjugation of the verbs there were twice as many different forms as there are in Modern English. The persons of the plural, for instance, differed in form from those of the singular: where we now say 'I *sing*, we *sing*, I *sang*, we *sang*,' the Old English forms were, 'ic *singe*, we *singath*, ic *sang*, we *sungon*.' The subjunctive mood, of which there are only a few traces left in modern English, occupied as prominent a place in Old English grammar as it does in Modern German.

Further, Old English differed from Modern English in being—like Modern German, but in a greater degree—comparatively free from words of foreign origin. It had, indeed, incorporated a certain number of Latin words, chiefly relating either to the institutions and ritual of the Church, or to things connected with Roman civilization. But these formed only a very small proportion of the entire vocabulary. Even for the technical terms of Christian theology, the Old English writers preferred, instead of adopting the Latin words that lay ready to their hand, to invent new equivalents, formed from native words by composition and derivation.

After what has been said, the reader will not be surprised to be told that a page, even of Old English prose, not to speak of the poetry, has quite the aspect of a foreign language. The following specimen is taken from a sermon by Ælfric, who died about A.D. 1025:

Thā the ne gelȳfath thurh āgenne cyre hī scoriath, nā thurh gewyrd; for-than-the gewyrd nis nān thing būton lēas wēna: ne nān thing sōthlīce be gewyrde ne gewyrth, ac ealle thing thurh Godes dōm bēoth geendebyrde, sē the cwæth thurh his wītegan, 'Ic āfandige manna heortan, and heora lendena, and ælcum sylle æfter his færelde, and āgenre āfundennysse.' Ne talige nan man his yfelan dǣda to Gode, ac talige ǣrest tō thām dēofle, the mancyn beswāc, and tō Adāmes forgǣgednysse; ac thēah swīthost tō him sylfum, thæt him yfel gelīcath, and ne līcath god.

They who do not believe refuse through their own choice, not through fate, because fate is nothing but a false notion; nor does anything truly come to pass by fate, but all things are ordered by the judgment of God, who said by his prophet, 'I try the hearts of men, and their reins, and give to every one according to his conduct, and according to his own device.' Let no man impute his evil deeds to God, but let him impute them first to the devil, who deceived mankind, and to Adam's transgression; but chiefly to himself, in that evil is pleasure to him and good pleases him not.

It is impossible here to give any complete rules for Old English pronunciation; but some approximate notion of the sounds of the language may be obtained by reading the above passage according to the following directions. Pronounce *y* and *ȳ* like the German *ü* or the French *u* (short and long), *æ* like *a* in 'hat,' *æ* like *e* in 'there,' and the other vowels like the italic letters in the words f*a*ther (*a* not marked is the same sound but shorter), b*e*d, v*ei*n, p*i*n, mach*i*ne, h*o*t, st*o*ne, p*u*t, r*u*le; pronounce *h* when not beginning a syllable like the German *ch,* and *f* in *gelyfath, yfel, deofle, sylfum,* as *v*. Sound *c* as *k,* except in *sothlice* and *ic,* in which the letter was pronounced as *ch* in 'church'; *sc* should be pronounced *sh*. The *g* in *agen, God, witegan, god* may be pronounced (though not quite correctly) as in the modern 'good'; in the other words in the extract it happens to have the less usual sound of *y* in 'young.' All other letters are to be pronounced as in modern English, and final *e* is always to be sounded.

It may be useful to append a few remarks on some of the words ocurring in the extract. *Thā* is the plural nominative of the demonstrative pronoun corresponding to our *that;* the nominative singular is *sē* (masc.), *sēo* (fem.), *thæt* (neut.); the word serves also as the definite article. *The* is an indeclinable relative, standing for 'who,' 'whom,' 'which.' In *ge-lȳf-ath* the middle syllable is the same as the second syllable in 'believe'; the verb *ge-lȳf-an* corresponds to the German *g-laub-en.* *Ne*, not, is in Old English put *before* the verb. With *thurh*, through, compare the German *durch.* *Āgenne* is accusative masculine singular of *āgen* own; compare the German *eigen.* *Cyre*, choice, is a masc. noun related to the verb *ceosan* to choose; the corresponding German word is *Kur.* *Hī*, they, is the plural of *hē.* *Scoriath* is the present tense plural of *scorian,* to refuse, a verb not preserved in modern English or German. *Nā*, here used for 'not,' is the modern provincial 'no' in 'that's *no* true.' *Ge-wyrd,* fate, is the word which in later English became 'weird.' *For-than-the,* because, is literally 'for-that-that.' *Nis* (=ne is) *nān thing,* 'is none thing'; in Old English two negatives did not 'make an affirmative,' but were combined for emphasis as in Greek. *Lēas,* false, lying; compare 'leasing,' falsehood, in the King James Bible. *Wēna,* opinion; connected with *wēnan,* to 'ween,' think. *Sōthlīce,* 'soothly,' truly; compare 'forsooth,' 'in good sooth.' *Gewyrth,* 3rd person sing. of *ge-weorthan* to take place, akin to the German *werden* to become. *Ac,* but; not found in modern English or German. *Ealle thing,* all things; the word *thing* had the nom. plural like the singular. *Cwæth,* the same word as 'quoth.' *Wītega,* prophet; the word existed also in old German, and was corrupted into *Weissager* (as if it meant 'wise-sayer'). *Āfandige,* from *āfandian,* to try. *Manna,* genitive plural of *mann.* *Heora,* genitive plural of *hē.* *Ælcum,* dative masc. sing. of *ælc,* now 'each.' *Sylle,* give, is the modern 'sell'; the word has changed its meaning. *Færelde,* dative of *færeld,* behaviour; connected with the verb 'to fare.' *Ā-funden-nyss* (dative *-nysse*), is from *āfunden* = Ger. *erfunden,* invented, with the ending *-nyss,* now *ness;* the word is fem., so that '*āgen-re*' (own) corresponds to the German '*eigen-er.*' *Talige,* from *talian,* to impute, count; compare 'tale.' *Ǣrest,* first = Ger. *erst. Mancyn,* mankind; the last part of the compound is our 'kin.' *Be-swāc,* past tense of *be-swīcan,* to deceive. *Thēah* is related to the modern English 'though' and the German *doch. Swīthost,* superlative of *swīthe,* strongly, very. *Tō him sylfum:* note the ending *-m* of the dative singular. *Ge-licath, līcath,* are identical with the modern verb 'to like,' the former having the prefix *ge-,* frequently occurring in Old English and German verbs.

4. OBJECT OF THIS BOOK.

The reader who has studied the foregoing pages with attention will have obtained a fairly correct notion of the general character of the language spoken by our ancestors a thousand or nine hundred years ago. The transformation of the English of King Alfred and Abbot Ælfric into the widely different language which we speak to-day has, as we have already said, been the result of gradual changes. We do not propose in this little volume to treat of these changes in their chronological sequence—to show, for instance, in what respects the English of Chaucer differs from that of Alfred, the English of Shakspere from that of Chaucer, and the English of the nineteenth century from that of the sixteenth. Information of this kind must be sought for in regular histories of the English language. Our purpose is merely to give some idea of the causes by which the more remarkable changes in the language were brought about, and to estimate the effect which these changes have had on its fitness as an instrument for the expression of thought.

One class of changes in English, though from some points of view immensely important, will be left almost entirely out of the present discussion. We refer to the alteration in pronunciation, which has been so great, that, even if the language had in all other respects continued the same, a speech delivered in the English of the tenth century would have been unintelligible to a hearer of to-day. Striking as the changes in pronunciation are, they have had no *direct* effect on the character of the language as a means of expression. Our meaning is neither better nor worse conveyed because, for instance, *stone, wine, foot, feet,* are no longer pronounced like the Old English *stān, wīn, fōt, fēt.* Still, there are *some* changes in pronunciation which have affected the expressive capacities of English indirectly, by causing other changes, or by obscuring the connexion of related words or forms; and these will need to be mentioned in order to explain the results which they have ultimately produced.

II

The Making of English Grammar

Great as are the differences between the grammar of Old
English and that of Modern English, the one has been
developed gradually out of the other. We propose now to
inquire into the causes to which this development has been
due. The questions which have to be answered are two.
First, why has the English language got rid of nearly all
the multitude of grammatical forms which it once possessed? Secondly, what new grammatical machinery has
the language acquired during the last thousand years, and
how was this new machinery obtained? These two questions cannot be kept entirely separate, because each of the
processes referred to—the disappearance of the older inflexions, and the development of new means of expressing
grammatical relations—has by turns been the cause and
the effect of the other. In some cases the dying out of the
ancient forms created a need which had to be supplied by
the invention of new modes of expression; in other cases
the old inflexions were dropped because they had become
superfluous, owing to the growth of other and more efficient means of indicating the functions of words in the
sentence. Nevertheless, it will conduce to lucidity to dis-

cuss the two questions, as far as possible, apart from each other.

1. SIMPLIFICATION OF ACCIDENCE.

The progressive reduction of the number of inflexional forms is a phenomenon not at all peculiar to English. On the contrary, most of the inflected languages of which the history is known have, to a greater or less extent, undergone the same kind of change. For example, although Modern High German is, as we have shown, much more complicated in its accidence than Modern English, it is much less so than the Old High German of a thousand years ago; the grammar of Old High German is simpler than that of Primitive Germanic, which was spoken at the beginning of the Christian era; and Primitive Germanic itself had retained only a comparatively small remnant of the profusion of inflexional forms possessed by the Primitive Indo-Germanic tongue, from which it was descended in common with Sanskrit, Greek, and Latin. We may note in passing that peasant German has lost much more of its original grammar than has the German spoken by educated people. This fact teaches us that culture is one of the influences which retard the process of simplification. But it should be remembered that culture may exist without books: there have been peoples in which there was little or no reading and writing, but in which nevertheless the arts of poetry and oratory were highly developed, and traditional correctness of speech was sedulously cultivated.

It is not wonderful that the tendency to simplification of accidence should be widely prevalent. Indeed, on a superficial view, we might naturally wonder that this tendency is not more conspicuously operative than is in fact the case. For even one's mother tongue obviously must require to be learnt; and nobody learns his mother tongue so perfectly as never to make any grammatical mistake. In a language with a great variety of conjugations and declensions, mistakes of grammar mostly consist in assimilating the inflexion of the less common words to the more familiar types. We might therefore expect that, between forgetfulness and the instinct for consistency, the rarer conjugations and declensions would always rapidly drop out of use, and that all inflexional languages would in a few generations approach perceptibly nearer to the ideal state in which the same grammatical relation should always be denoted by the same change in the form of a word.

But in all matters of language the influence of tradition is extremely powerful. The mistakes or intentional innovations in grammar made by individuals are for the most part condemned by the community at large, and only few of them come to affect the general language. Probably most English children have sometimes said 'mouses' or 'speaked,' but these regularized forms do not appear in the speech of even illiterate adults. So the tendency to grammatical simplification in languages is usually slow in its working, unless it happens to be stimulated by some special cause.

Among the causes which hasten the progress of languages towards grammatical simplicity, there are two that require particular notice. There are (1) phonetic change; and (2) the mixture of peoples speaking different languages, or different dialects of the same language.

Phonetic Change.

When we study the history of any language, we always

discover that, at some period or other, certain of its elementary sounds—certain 'letters,' as we might call them, of its spoken alphabet—have undergone an alteration in pronunciation. The changes to which we here refer are unconscious and unintentional, and are so very gradual that it would need an acute and attentive ear to discern any difference between the sound of a word uttered by young men and by old men living at one time. But when, as is often the case, the pronunciation of a vowel or consonant becomes in each successive generation a little more unlike what it was at first, the total amount of change may in time be very great. If we could compare (by means of a phonograph or otherwise) the present pronunciation of some language with its pronunciation a few centuries ago, we might find, for instance, that all the *a*'s had turned into *o*'s, or all the *d*'s into *t*'s, or *vice versa*. More commonly, we should find that a particular vowel or consonant had changed into a certain other vowel or consonant whenever it occurred in the same part of a word (beginning, middle, or end); or whenever it came in an accented syllable; or whenever it came next to a certain other sound, or to any sound of a certain class; and that under other conditions it had either undergone a different kind of change, or else had remained unaltered.

The term 'phonetic change' is conventionally restricted to that kind of unconscious alteration of sounds which has just been described. If we study any particular language as it is spoken to-day, and ascertain what sound in it represents each of the sounds of some older form of the language under each of the varieties of condition under which it occurred, we shall obtain a body of rules which are called the *phonetic laws* of the present stage of the language. It is often said that the phonetic laws applicable to one and the same dialect and date have no exceptions whatever. Whether this is absolutely true or not, it is so nearly true that whenever we meet with a seeming exception we shall be pretty safe in believing that there has been at work some other process than 'phonetic change' in the sense above explained. For instance, it is not a case of phonetic change that we say 'I broke,' where our ancestors said 'I brake.' What has happened is not that *a* has changed into *o*, but that the old past tense has been superseded by a new one, imitated from the participle *broken*. Again, an apparent exception to a phonetic law may be due to the fact that one dialect has borrowed a form from another dialect in which the course of phonetic change had been different.

Why a particular phonetic change should take place in one language, dialect, or period and not in another is a question on which we cannot here enter. For our present purpose, it is enough to note the fact that the same original sound may develop quite differently in two dialects of the same language, and that a sound may continue for many centuries unaltered, and then enter on a course of rapid change.

The results of phonetic change, so far as they affect the history of grammar, are of three kinds:

1. *Confluent development.* Sometimes two originally different sounds come to be represented in a later stage of the language by a single sound.

Thus the Old English $\bar{a}$ and $\breve{o}$ (in certain positions) have yielded the Modern English $\bar{o}$, so that *hāl* (whole) and *fŏla* (foal) now form a perfect rime.

2. *Divergent development.* One and the same original

sound may, owing to difference of conditions, yield two or more distinct sounds in the later language.

Thus in Old English *ic lǽde,* I lead, and *ic lǽdde,* I led, had the same vowel; but because in one word the vowel was followed by a single and in the other by a double *d,* their modern forms have different vowels.

3. *Dropping of sounds.* In some cases the phonetic law relating to a particular vowel or consonant is that, when it occurs under certain conditions, it will neither remain unchanged nor change into anything else, but will vanish altogether.

Thus, an Old French *t,* if it comes at the end of a word, becomes silent in Modern French. Again, every short vowel which ended a word (of more than one syllable) in Old English has long ago dropped off, so that all the words which a thousand years ago were disyllables with short vowel endings are now monosyllables.

Now supposing that in any language the sounds which happen to be subject to these three kinds of phonetic change are those which are used in the inflexional endings, it is obvious that the result must be a considerable up-setting of the grammatical system. The effect, however, is not immediately to produce simplification. On the contrary, the tendency of 'divergent development' is to increase the number of declensions and conjugations, because the same original termination becomes different in different words. The effect of 'confluent development' and 'dropping of sounds' is to make the inflexional system less efficient for its purpose by confounding different cases, persons, tenses, etc., under the same form. It is owing to changes of this sort in prehistoric times that the Latin language has the awkward defect of having only one form

(*Musae*) for the genitive and dative singular and the nominative and vocative plural of certain nouns. The same cause, also, accounts for the inconvenient peculiarity of Old English grammar, in having a large number of nouns with their nominative singular and nominative plural alike. This example is instructive, because it shows the fallacy of the notion sometimes maintained, that phonetic change does not destroy inflexions till they have already become useless. In what may be called prehistoric continental English, the plural ending of many neuter nouns was *ŭ*. There came a time when it became a phonetic law that a final *ŭ* always dropped off when it followed a heavy syllable, but remained after a light syllable. Hence in Old English as we know it the plural of *scip* (ship) was *scipu,* but the plural of *hūs* (house) was *hūs,* just like the singular. In this instance phonetic change produced two different effects: it made two declensions out of one, and it deprived a great many words of a useful inflexional distinction.

We thus see that the *direct* result of phonetic change on the grammar of a language is chiefly[1] for evil: it makes it more complicated and less lucid. But when these inconveniences become too great to be endured, they provoke a reaction. The speakers of the language find out how to express needful grammatical distinctions by other than inflexional means; or else they generalize the use of those inflexional forms that have happened to escape decay, applying them to other words than those to which they originally belonged. In this way phonetic change leads in-

---

[1] Not exclusively so; for it may hasten the disappearance of inconvenient forms which traditional inertia might otherwise have retained after better modes of expression had come into existence.

directly to that kind of simplification which we shall find exemplified in the history of the English language.

Mixture of Peoples.

The second condition which we mentioned as favouring grammatical simplification was the mixture of peoples speaking different languages or dialects.

Let it be imagined that an island inhabited by people speaking a highly inflected language receives a large accession of foreigners to its population. To make the case as simple as possible, let it be further imagined that there is no subsequent communication with the outside world, and that nobody on the island can read or write. What may be expected to happen?

It is a matter of general experience that a person who tries to learn a foreign language entirely by conversation finds the vocabulary easier to acquire than the grammar. And it is wonderful how well, for the common purposes of intercourse, one can often get on in a foreign country by using the bare stems of words, without any grammar at all. Many Englishmen of the uneducated class have lived for years in Germany, and managed to make themselves fairly well understood, without ever troubling themselves with the terminations of adjectives or articles, or the different ways of forming the plural in nouns. In our imaginary island the foreigners will soon pick up a stock of words; if the island language is like the Germanic ones, in which the main stress is never on the inflexional syllables, their task will be much easier. The grammatical endings will be learnt more slowly, and only the most striking will be learnt at all. The natives will soon manage to understand the broken jargon of the newcomers, and to adopt it in conversation with them, avoiding the use of those inflexions which they discover to be puzzling to their hearers. But if they acquire the habit of using a simplified grammar in their dealings with foreigners, they will not entirely escape using it in their intercourse with each other. If there is intermarriage and absorption of the strangers in the native population, the language of the island must in a few generations be deprived of a considerable number of its inflexional forms.

Let us now consider a somewhat different case. Suppose that the two peoples that live together and blend into one, instead of speaking widely distinct languages, speak dialects not too far apart to allow of a good deal of mutual understanding from the first, or at any rate as soon as the ear has been accustomed to the constant differences of pronunciation. The two dialects, let us suppose, have a large common vocabulary, with marked differences in inflexion—a very frequent case, because phonetic change is apt to cause greater divergences in the unstressed endings than in the stressed stems of words. The result will be much the same as when peoples speaking distinct languages are mingled; indeed there are reasons for thinking that the change will be even more rapid and decisive. For one thing, the blending of the two peoples is likely to take place more quickly. Then, as the speakers of neither dialect will be disposed to take the other as their model of correct speech, two different sets of inflexional forms will for a time be current in the same district, and there will arise a hesitation and uncertainty about the grammatical endings that will tend to render them indistinct in pronunciation, and hence not worth preserving.

We see, therefore, that the simplification of the inflexional machinery of a language is powerfully stimulated by the absorption of large bodies of foreigners into the population and by the mixture of different dialects. It has now to be shown how far these causes were actually in operation during the formative period of the English language.

The Angles, Saxons, and Jutes, who settled in Britain in the fifth and sixth centuries, though speaking substantially the same language, brought with them their peculiarities of dialect. They established themselves independently in different parts of the country; and, in consequence of local separation, their original divergences of speech gradually bcame wider, so that in three or four centuries the kinds of English spoken in Wessex, Mercia, Kent, and Northumbria, had become markedly different; and each of these dialectal areas doubtless included several minor varieties of local speech. In the main, the Old English dialects seem to have differed but little in their vocabulary, and the diversity of pronunciation, though considerable, was not sufficient often to disguise the identity of the words. Except for the grammatical differences, a Kentishman and a Northumbrian of the eighth century would probably find it easier to understand each other's speech than their rustic descendants do at the present day. The increase of population, and the establishment of political unity over larger and larger areas during the succeeding centuries, necessarily resulted in the formation of mixed dialects, and this contributed to the decay of the inflexional system of the language.

A further impulse in the same direction was given by the conquests and settlements of the Danes and Northmen, which fill so large a space in the annals of England from the ninth to the eleventh century. The vast importance of those events is perhaps not adequately appreciated by ordinary readers of history. What we are accustomed to regard as the history of England during these centuries is really little more than the history of *English* England; the larger portion of England which was under Scandinavian rule had no chroniclers. Of the Danish dynasty which reigned at York we know hardly more than the names of the kings; and the history of Danish East Anglia and Mercia is even more obscure. It is only by the indirect evidence of place-names and modern dialects that we learn that in some districts of England the population must at one time have been far more largely Scandinavian than English, and that important Scandinavian settlements existed in almost every county north of the Thames. In the year 1016 Cnut of Denmark conquered the throne of England, and his strong rule gave to the country a degree of political unity such as it had never had before. Under the succeeding kings, even under the Englishman Edward the Confessor, the highest official posts in the kingdom continued to be held by men of Danish origin. The result of these new conditions was the extension of Scandinavian influence to those parts of the country which had previously been most purely English.

The language spoken by the Danes and Northmen was an older form of that in which the Icelandic sagas were written. It was so nearly like Old English that a Scandinavian settler in England would very soon learn to understand the speech of his neighbours, so far as the mere word-stems were concerned. After a little experience of English habits of pronunciation, he would be able to recognise most of the words as identical with those of his native tongue. The grammatical inflexions, however, would be more puzzling, many of them being quite dissimilar in the two languages. Under such conditions there must have arisen mixed dialects, mainly English, but containing many

Danish words, and characterized by the dropping or confused use of some of the terminations distinctive of cases, genders, and persons. We possess, in fact, one short specimen of Old English as it was written by a Dane. This is an inscription at Aldborough in Yorkshire, which has been read as follows: *Ulf lēt ārǣran cyrice for hanum and for Gunware saula,* i.e., 'Ulf caused a church to be built for himself and for the soul of Gunwaru.' Probably the sentence is more correct Old English than Ulf habitually spoke; but he has made the mistake of putting the Danish pronoun *hanum* instead of the English *him*. It is a pity that we have no more actual examples to show what Danish-English was like in the eleventh century. But since we know for a fact that those districts in which the Danes had settled are precisely those in which English grammar became simplified most rapidly, there can be no doubt that the Scandinavian admixture in the population was *one* of the causes that contributed to bring about the disuse of the Old English inflexions.

After the Scandinavian settlements, the next great event that affected the development of the English language was the Norman Conquest. It is not likely that the great political change of A.D. 1066 had any marked immediate effect on the actual speech of the people. It is, however, certain that the grammar of the *literary* language began to show very striking changes early in the twelfth century. The ending *-an* of the southern dialect came to be written *-en*, and all the inflexional endings consisting in vowels were reduced to a uniform *-e*. The explanation is, no doubt, that the indistinctness in the pronunciation of the endings, which had gradually invaded the popular language, now manifested itself in writing. When the monasteries, the homes of the literary class, were filled with foreign monks, the superiors in education of their native brethren, the vernacular culture could not but suffer. The traditional orthography ceased to be maintained, and there was less and less solicitude for traditional correctness of expression on the part of the writers. Hence, in all probability, the alteration in the language between 1066 and 1150 appears from the literary remains more rapid than it actually was.[2]

While, however, the apparent immediate effect of the Conquest on the English language is partly an illusion, there is no doubt that that event did introduce a new influence which operated with great, and for two centuries constantly increasing, effect. Under the Norman and Angevin kings there was a great influx of Frenchmen into the country. The language of the court and the nobility was French; amongst the middle classes every one who aspired to social consideration endeavoured to become fluent in the fashionable language. In the grammar-schools boys were, even down to the fourteenth century, taught their Latin through the medium of French. The writing and reading of English, apparently, almost entirely ceased to be a part of regular school teaching, for many of the extant early Middle English manuscripts were written by persons who evidently had never learnt to spell their native language, but rendered the words phonetically according to the French values of the letters. In the thirteenth century it would seem that a very considerable portion of the population of England must have been bilingual. How far-reaching the effect of the foreign influence was at this period

[2] The probability of this view is confirmed by a study of *Domesday Book*. This record, compiled in 1086, contains thousands of English names of persons and places, written phonetically by Norman scribes. The forms exhibit the changes above referred to with a uniformity that does not appear in the spelling of native writers until about a century later.

may be seen from the large number of Old French words that have found their way into our rustic dialects.

From what has already been said, it will be evident that the natural tendency of this condition of things would be to promote the disuse of the traditional inflexional system of English. It is impossible to determine to what extent the actual change which took place in this direction is to be ascribed to the use of a foreign language by the side of the vernacular, because we have no means of measuring the efficiency of the other powerful causes which were working to the same result. But that the change, at least in the southern part of the kingdom, was materially accelerated by this agency there seems to be no reasonable doubt.

It is now time to turn from generalities to the consideration of some specific instances of the simplification which has taken place in English accidence. We will begin with the declension of substantives.

Old English had many declensions of substantives—how many we can hardly say, because it is not the custom to denote them by numbers as is done in Latin and Greek grammar, and scholars might find it difficult to decide what amount of variation should be regarded as constituting a separate 'declension.' However, there was one declension which formed its genitive singular in -es and its nominative (and accusative) plural in -as; and there were other declensions in which -a, -an, -e appear as endings for the genitive singular, and -a, -an, -e, -u for the nominative plural; and yet others in which the genitive singular or the nominative plural, or both, were like the nominative singular, or different from it in only the vowel of the root syllable. Out of all these the -es and -as declension is the only one that remains in general use. Except for a few irregular plurals, all modern English substantives are declined with

the endings (written -'s and -es or -s) which descend from
the Old English -es and -as.

Now this is obviously an instance of the famous principle
of 'survival of the fittest.' For amongst the Old English
case-endings -es was the only one that never meant anything
else than a genitive singular, and -as was the only one that
never meant anything else than a nominative or accusative
plural. Thus, *hanan* stood for the genitive, dative, and
accusative of *hana,* a cock; *gife* might be either genitive,
dative, or accusative singular, and *gifa* either nominative,
accusative, or genitive plural, of *gifu* a gift; and so forth.

It is a popular error to suppose that it was in consequence of the Norman Conquest that the -es and -as declension came to supersede all the rest. In fact the change
began much earlier; and it began in the northern dialect.
For this there were special reasons.

We have just seen that the noun-declension of southern
Old English (from which our examples were taken) was
full of ambiguities; the reason being that the inherited
Germanic case-endings, originally distinct, had undergone
phonetic change to such an extent that many of them had
come to coincide in form. In the northern dialect the state
of things was still worse, because in that dialect the termination -an regularly dropped its nasal; and further, the
mixture of different local varieties of speech had led to
a general indistinctness and uncertainty in the pronunciation of those vowels which served as case-endings, so that
in some words the terminations -a, -æ, -e, -o, and -u seem to
be used indiscriminately in the same text. As an instance
of the greater imperfection of the noun-declension in
Northumbrian as compared with southern Old English,
we may refer to the word 'eye.' In the southern dialect
the nominative and accusative singular were *ēage,* the geni-

tive and dative singular and the nominative and accusative plural were *ēagan*. But in the northern dialect *ēgo* is found for all these cases.

In the Durham Gospels, written about the middle of the tenth century, we may see how this state of confusion had already begun to be remedied. The old declensions still survived; but when there was need for greater distinctness of expression than the old forms afforded, the endings *-es* for the genitive and *-as* for the plural nominative were sub-stituted for those of other declensions. Accordingly, many of the substantives which in West Saxon (*i.e.* southern Old English) belong to other declensions have in the Durham Book occasionally, though not exclusively, the *-es* and *-as* forms. On the following page is a table showing a few com-parative specimens of the inflexion in the two dialects, the new forms being indicated by italics.

It is true that in the Northumbrian dialect of the tenth century the substitution of *-es* and *-as* for the other equiva-lent terminations had merely begun. But a change which constituted so great an improvement in distinctiveness of expression could not fail to go on. Before three centuries had passed, it had extended itself to nearly all substantives. The increased intercourse between the different parts of the country, which was the result of the political unifica-tion of England, led to the introduction of these northern forms, recommended by their superior clearness, into the grammar of the midland dialects, from which our modern literary English is descended. To some extent, however, the advantage which the language had gained by the reduction of its many declensions to one was lost by the effect of phonetic change. The tendency to increase the propor-tionate stress on the body of the word, and consequently to obscure the pronunciation of the endings, caused the origi-

	WEST SAXON.			NORTHUMBRIAN.			
	Nom. Sing.	*Gen. Sing.*	*Nom. Pl.*	*Nom. Sing.*	*Gen. Sing.*	*Nom. Pl.*	
	culfre	culfran	culfran	culfra, culfre	——	culfero, *culfras*	dove
	eorthe	eorthan	——	eortho	eorthu, *eorthes*	——	earth
	gītsung	gītsunge	gītsunga	gītsung	gītsunges	gītsungas	covetousness
	heorte	heortan	heortan	hearta	*heartes*	hearto	heart
	līchoma	līchoman	līchoman	līchoma	līchoma, *līchomes*	līchoma, līchomo	body
	lufu	lufe	——	lufa	lufæ, *lufes*	——	love
	miht	mihte	mihta	mæht	*mæhtes*	mæhto, mæhta	might
	mōdor	mōdor	mōdor	mōdor	mōder, *mōderes*	mōdero	mother
	steorra	steorran	steorran	stearra	*stearres*	*stearras*	star
	thēowe	thēowan	thēowan	thīwa	*thīuæs*	*thīuwas*	maidservant
	wuduwe	wuduwan	wuduwan	widwa	*widwes*	widwa	widow
	wītega	wītegan	wītegan	wītga	wītgo, -ga, *wītges*	wītgo, -ga, *wītgas*	prophet

nal -es and -as to be pronounced alike. Hence in Middle English *kinges,* for example, stood for both the genitive singular and the nominative plural of *king.*

In southern Old English, the system of noun-inflexion, though somewhat better than that of the northern dialect, was still, as we have seen, so imperfect that most of its forms were inadequate to indicate with certainty the case and number of a word. It became still more defective when— as happened in the twelfth century—all the vowels of the inflexional endings came to be represented by one indistinct sound, represented by the letter *e,* and when, moreover, many monosyllabic nominatives became disyllabic by the addition of a final -*e* due to assimilation to other cases. The defects of the system were obviated to some extent by applying the suffix -*en,* which was inherited in words like *sterren* from *sterre* star, to form the genitive and the plural of words in which the regular case-endings were ambiguous. There was, in fact, a definite movement in early southern Middle English towards making -*en* the regular plural ending of nouns. We find in the thirteenth century such forms as *trewen,* trees (where Old English had *treowu*), *schoon,* shoes (Old English *sceōs*), *lambren,* lambs, *calveren,* calves, *eyren,* eggs (Old English *lambru, cealfru, ǣgru*). This tendency was arrested in the fourteenth century by the spread of the -*es* forms from the midland dialects. But the rustic speech of the south-western counties has still a few plurals like *housen* (Old English *hūs*); and modern standard English says *children* (Old English *cildru, cild,* modern northern and north midland dialects *childer*), and in more or less old-fashioned diction also *brethren* (Old English *brōthor, brōthru,* Old Norse *brǣthr*) and *kine* (Old English *cȳ,* modern Scotch and northern dialects *kye*). It is somewhat curious that al-

though, as we have seen, the original *-n* as a plural ending
had already been lost in the Northumbrian dialect of the
tenth century, the modern Scotch plurals of *ox* and *eye* are
ousen and *een;* and it is still more curious that in Scotch
and in most provincial dialects the plural of *shoe* is *shoon,*
though in all varieties of Old English it was *sceōs.* The
anomaly, however, like other anomalies in language, is
capable of explanation. The genitive plural of *oxa* in Old
Northumbrian was *oxna,* and that of *ēgo* (eye) was *ēgna.*
The need for making a formal difference between singular
and plural in these words was supplied by transferring the
n from the genitive to the nominative plural. As for the
word *shoe,* it ended in a vowel; and as most other monosyllabic nouns with vowel endings made the genitive plural
in *-na,* this word was assimilated in declension to the words
which it resembled in form.

It may at first sight appear strange, seeing that the Middle
English *-es* has come so near to being the universal plural
ending, that the process has not been carried to its limit,
and that we have still our half-score of 'irregular plurals.'
But the desire for uniformity has had a very small share in
the evolution of English grammar. The changes that have
taken place, where they are not due to the operation of
phonetic law, have mostly been produced either by the
attempt to avoid ambiguity, or by the disposition to save
time or trouble in speaking. Now the plurals *men, teeth,
geese, mice, lice, oxen,* are unambiguous in form; if we
were to substitute the 'regular' forms, they would to the
ear be identical with the genitives, *man's, tooth's, goose's,*
and so on. Moreover, the irregular plurals are all either
shorter or easier to pronounce than the regular forms
would be. There were thus two good reasons for not assimilating the declension of these words to the prevailing type.

It is true that a few of the plurals anciently formed by vowel-change have not survived: for instance, where Old English had *bōc, bēc,* we now say *book, books.* But if *bēc* had come down into modern English, it would by phonetic law have become *beech,*[3] which would have had the double disadvantage of not showing its relationship to the singular, and of coinciding in form with a quite different word.

There remain to be noticed two or three points in the history of the simplification in the declension of substantives. For the genitive plural the Old English endings were, according to the declension, *-a* and *-ena.* The latter, as the more distinct and unambiguous, had already in Old English begun to encroach on the territory of the former; and in early Middle English this movement was continued, *-ene* (two syllables) being in monosyllabic nouns generally preferred to *-e.* Thus we have *kingene king* for 'king of kings.' With longer words this ending was too unwieldy, and speakers seem early to have fallen into the habit of using the plural nominative form (at first in disyllabic nouns, afterwards in others) as a genitive. Thus the one form *king-es,* which already had three functions, expressing the genitive singular and the nominative and accusative plural, came to stand for the genitive plural as well. Ambiguity was for a time prevented by the inflexion of the accompanying article or adjective. But in the end these parts of speech lost their case-endings, and the result was that a form like *horses* had nothing to show whether it stood for a genitive singular or a nominative, accusative, or genitive plural. This remains as a real defect in modern spoken English, though in writing we obviate it by a device of recent origin,

---

[3] Because the same cause that turned *ō* into *ē* had also altered the pronunciation of the *c.*

using *horses* for the nominative (and accusative) plural, *horse's* for the genitive singular, and *horses'* for the genitive plural. The weakness in our system of inflexions would have been seriously inconvenient, if it had not been for the introduction of the practice of using the preposition *of* instead of the genitive inflexion—an innovation respecting which we shall afterwards have to speak.

Besides the genitive, Old English had two other inflected cases, the accusative and the dative. But phonetic change had already made such havoc with the original Germanic endings that even in southern Old English the accusative and nominative were always alike in the plural, and very frequently, perhaps most frequently, in the singular also. In the northern dialect the formal difference between the cases, in substantives, had almost disappeared. When a case-distinction has become a mere occasional irregularity, the speakers of the language have learnt to do without it, and have no motive for resisting the influences that tend to abolish it. The fact that the articles and adjectives were inflected rendered the accusative ending of substantives less necessary; and with the growing habit of placing the parts of a sentence in one uniform order, the subject and object could be quite well distinguished without the aid of inflexions. Hence the accusative, as an inflected case of substantives, disappeared early in Middle English. The dative lasted longer; in fact we have some faint traces of it still. In Old English the dative singular ended in -*e* or (rarely) in -*a,* and in one large class of words in -*an;* in Middle English these endings became -*e* and -*en.* The ending of the dative plural was -*um,* but this was weakened in late Old English into -*on* and -*an,* becoming -*en* in Middle English.[4]

4 The same change has occurred in German, where -*en* or -*n* is now the universal ending of the dative plural.

As the case of the indirect object the dative did not survive long in Middle English, but when governed by prepositions it retained its endings down to the fourteenth century. In the latter part of that century—for instance, in the writings of Chaucer—the dative endings rarely appear except in phrases that had become adverbs, such as *on live,* which has in modern English been shortened to 'alive.' The reason why *alive* has a *v,* while *life* has an *f,* is that the Old English *f* between vowels was pronounced *v.* Hence, while the Old English nominative *līf* is represented in modern English by 'life,' its dative *līfe* is represented by the last syllable of 'alive.' There is one dative plural surviving in modern English, the adverb *whilom.* Here the Old English form -*um* still remains, not even having undergone the Middle English alteration to -*en;* an instance of the important fact that some peculiarity in the *meaning* of a word will occasionally cause it to be exempted from the normal effect of phonetic change.

The case-inflexion of pronouns is more permanent than that of nouns. As any personal pronoun is far more frequent in use than any individual noun, the use of the case-distinction in pronouns is more a matter of fixed habit. But already in Old English the dative and accusative had become alike for the pronouns of the first and second persons in both numbers; and in Middle English these two cases became confused together also in the third person. A fact not very easy to account for is that it was the dative and not the accusative form that finally prevailed.[5] Our modern 'objectives,' *him, her, 'em,* represent the Old Eng-

[5] The explanation may perhaps be that pronouns referring to persons occurred more frequently in the case of the indirect object than in that of the direct object. The 'objective' case of the neuter *it* (Old English *hit*) is *it,* from the accusative, not *him* from the dative.

lish datives *him, hire, heom*. The Old English masculine
accusative *hine* survives only in the *'un* ('I see 'un') of the
south-western dialects.

We now come to what is the most remarkable, and one
of the most beneficial, of all the changes which the English language has undergone—the substitution of 'natural'
for 'grammatical' gender. It is not easy for us English
people to understand what a wonderful change this really
was. We are apt to look on it as the most natural thing
in the world that 'gender' should correspond to sex: that
masculine and feminine nouns should be those denoting
males and females respectively, and that neuter nouns
should be those which denote objects which are not regarded as possessing sex[6]. And yet this state of things
cannot be so *very* natural; for the fact is that English is the
only language, among those that are at all generally known,
in which it exists. In Sanskrit, Greek, Latin (and its descendants, French, Italian, Spanish, Portuguese), German,
Dutch, Swedish, Danish, Welsh, Irish, Russian, and innumerable other languages, gender (at least with regard
to names of inanimate things), is a mere useless classifica-
tion of nouns; that is to say, it expresses no distinctions in
thought. So it was in all dialects of English, so far as we
know, as late as the year 1000. But two centuries later, the

[6] In absolute strictness, we ought to say that in modern English the masculine and feminine genders are restricted to nouns denoting persons, or things
in which we see some analogy to personality, while the neuter gender
applies to designations of things not regarded as personal. A personified
abstraction is regarded imaginatively as male or female, and is spoken of
as 'he' or 'she' accordingly; so, too, with certain material objects, as the
sun, the moon, a ship. On the other hand, a baby, or an animal, may be
called 'it' instead of 'he' or 'she,' when not distinctly regarded as a personal being. In the latter case, the absence of a common-gender pronoun
causes us to avail ourselves of the liberty of using the neuter gender more
frequently than we otherwise should.

'Ormulum,' a metrical harmony of the Gospels written in the East Midland dialect, shows that gender had come to be entirely dependent on meaning. Instead of being a useless complication in the grammar, it had become a valuable means of expression.

This unique and momentous change, completed, so far as one dialect is concerned, in a space of two centuries, evidently requires to be accounted for. It is closely connected with another change of which we find evidence in the same text. The disuse of inflexion, which we have seen to be a natural consequence of the admixture of a foreign element in the population, had in the Danish part of England gone so far that the adjective had ceased to mark gender or case by difference of termination; and the article *the* was used indeclinably just as in modern English. Hence the gender of a noun had no other effect on the sentence than that of determining the choice of the pronoun referring to it. As the inflexional reminders no longer existed, the traditional gender of the nouns was easily forgotten, and the pronouns *he, she,* and *it* came to be used with strict reference to the *meaning* of the nouns for which they were substitutes.

The East Midland dialect, as has been already said, is the ancestor of our modern literary English. The southern dialects kept up the old unmeaning genders, and the inflexion of the adjective and article, to some extent down to the fourteenth century. Perhaps the final disappearance of 'grammatical' gender, for which there were many causes, was promoted by the extensive use of the French language in England; at any rate instances have been found in Early Middle English in which the gender of nouns is assimilated to that of their French synonyms. The uncertainty thus arising would naturally strengthen the tendency to adopt the significant gender of the East Midland dialect.

In the writings of Chaucer, which extend to the end of the fourteenth century, the adjective, though no longer inflected for gender and case, still retains some traces of its grammatical endings. The plural was marked by a final *e;* and an adjective also took a final *e* when preceded by an article or other defining word.

But in the following century these endings quickly disappeared, in obedience to a tendency which is the most conspicuous feature in the later development of English grammar, the tendency to reduce the number of syllables in words wherever it was possible. The movement towards monosyllabism continued even into the nineteenth century. Within the memory of living persons it was the rule in reading the Bible or the Liturgy to make two syllables of words like *loved* and *changed,* which are now most commonly pronounced in one syllable. The shortening tendency has so widely prevailed that every short vowel that ended a word in Old English has dropped off. In Chaucer's English the various forms of the verb 'to love' were all disyllables: *(to) loven* or *(to) lovë, (I) lovë, (we) loven, (I) lovedë, (we) loveden.* In modern English the only parts of the verb that are not monosyllables are *loving,* and the archaic *lovest, loveth, lovedst.* Although our grammar is almost entirely of East Midland origin, the form *loveth* which belonged to that dialect has been displaced by the northern form *loves,* which had the recommendation of being more easily contracted into a monosyllable.

As we have already remarked, the simplification of English grammar has not been in any considerable degree due to the desire for uniformity. If such a desire had been characteristic of the English mind, we should certainly have got rid of the complicated system of strong verbs: but in spite of the many changes which that system has undergone in detail, it remains just as intricate as it was in Old English. One reason is that the strong preterites *gave, shook, came, rode,* and the like, are easier to pronounce than *gived, shaked, comed, rided.* The instinct for regularity has been too feeble to overcome the resistance of tradition when supported by the preference for the phonetically easier form. It is true that a few verbs that were strong in Old English are now 'regular'; but there are quite as many instances of contrary change. In the modern *dug* and *stuck* (formerly *digged, sticked*), we have actually a new strong conjugation. The modern forms, it may be noted, are easier to pronounce than the old ones.

There is, however, one point in the conjugation of verbs which does exhibit the influence of the tendency to uniformity. In Old English most of the strong preterites had different vowels in the singular and plural, as in *ic sang, wē sungon.* This was the case also in Middle English; but the fact that in modern English the weak preterite has the same form for singular and plural has led to the disappearance of the distinction in the strong verbs also; we use *sang* in both cases. The second person singular had in Old English strong verbs the same vowel as the plural, and had an ending different from that of the weak verbs: *thū sunge, thū lufodest.* In modern English the old form has been superseded by *sangest,* after the analogy of the weak verbs.

The only feature in the simplification of English accidence that remains to be mentioned is the disappearance of the subjunctive mood. In Old English the subjunctive played as important a part as in modern German, and was used in much the same way. Its inflexion differed in several respects from that of the indicative. The only formal trace of the old subjunctive still remaining, except the use of *be* and *were,* is the omission of the final *s* in the third person singular of verbs. And even this is rapidly dropping out of use, its only remaining function being to emphasize the uncertainty of a supposition. Perhaps in another generation the subjunctive forms will have ceased to exist except in the single instance of *were,* which serves a useful function, although we manage to dispense with a corresponding form in other verbs.

2. NEW GRAMMATICAL MATERIAL

The disappearance of the Old English inflexions is only half the story of the development of English grammar. A considerable amount of new grammatical material has been introduced, to serve the needs of expression in cases where the old machinery has become inefficient through phonetic change and other causes, or where it was from the beginning inadequate for its purpose.

We have now to see from what sources this new material was derived, and what were the necessities which led to its adoption.

It is not very often that a language enriches its grammatical system by adoption from other tongues; but owing to the peculiar circumstances of English its history presents a few examples of this rare phenomenon. In Old English the personal pronouns of the third person were as follows:

	SINGULAR.			PLURAL.
	Masculine.	*Feminine.*	*Neuter.*	
Nominative	hē	hēo, hĭe, hī	hit	hĭe, hī
Accusative	hine	hĭe, hī	hit	hĭe, hī
Genitive	his	hire	his	heora
Dative	him	hire	him	heom

It will be seen from this table that the words 'he,' 'she,' and 'they' were very nearly alike; and in the process of phonetic change they came to be represented in southern Middle English by the form *he*.[7] In the same way, the single form *here* came to stand both for 'her' (genitive and dative) and for 'their.' This ambiguity of forms was a defect which the language had no means of remedying from its own resources. But it so happened that in parts of England which were largely inhabited by Danes the native pronouns were supplanted by the Scandinavian pronouns which are represented by the modern *she*,[8] *they, them, their*. These forms, recommended by their superior clearness, gradually made their way from their original home in the north and the north-east midlands into the dialects of the rest of England. Their progress, however, was not very rapid: Chaucer uses *she*, but his *her* serves for the genitive, dative, and accusative of the feminine singular and the genitive plural. This is much the same state of things as exists in modern German, where *ihr Haus* may be either 'her house' or 'their house' (*Ihr Haus*, written with a capital *I*, but pronounced in the same way, is 'your house'), and *ihr* may also mean 'to her' and 'you.' Perhaps the want of distinction between the pronouns did not often occasion any actual misunderstanding, but clearly the introduction of the Danish forms was a real improvement.

[7] In the dialects of the south-western counties *he* is still used for the feminine as well as for the masculine pronoun. "He is their mother" is one of the many examples quoted in the *English Dialect Dictionary*.

[8] The origin of this pronoun is unexplained, but the fact that *they, them, their* represent Scandinavian demonstrative pronouns favours the hypothesis that *she* is connected in some obscure way with the Old Norse feminine demonstratives *sū* and *siā*, which had often the function of personal pronouns.

In some other points English has found means to improve its pronouns without calling in foreign aid. One defect of the Old English pronominal system was that *his* was both masculine and neuter. While gender was merely 'grammatical' this did not greatly matter. But when gender became significant, people began to feel that the use of *his* referring to inanimate things involved a sort of personification. We see traces of this feeling in the King James Bible of 1611, where *his* is the ordinary genitive of *it* (or, as for this date it is perhaps more correct to say, the corresponding possessive pronoun), but *her* is sometimes used where it was felt that a male personification would be very inappropriate. Still earlier (in 1534), we find Tindale writing: "If salt have loste hyr saltnes, what shall be seasoned ther with?" In North West Midland writings we find *it* (*hit*) used as a possessive pronoun as early as the fourteenth century, and this use is still common in dialects. The first writer, so far as is known, to append the regular possessive ending to *it* was the foreigner, Florio, who uses *its* in 1598, and several times in his later works. Shakspere has one or two examples of the possessive *it* ("Go to *it* grandam, and *it* grandam shall give it a plum"), and in those plays which exist only in editions published after his death *its* occurs a few times. The Bible of 1611 has no *its;* in one passage (Lev. xxv. 5) we read "that groweth of *it* own accord," but in the modern editions *its* has been substituted. The use of *its* became general in the seventeenth century, but for a long time there seems to have been a feeling that the older *his* or *her* was more dignified.

Another beneficial change in English pronouns was due to the accident that—in accordance with the tendency towards shortening of which we have before spoken—the final *n* in unemphatic monosyllables was often dropped.

(Examples may be seen in the indefinite article *a,* which is an unemphatic form of the numeral *one,* and in *i', o'* for *in* and *on.*) It was this circumstance that produced the difference between the forms of the same pronoun in 'This is *my* book' and 'This book is *mine.*' It is true that the full forms *mine* and *thine* long continued to be used before a noun beginning with a vowel or *h,* as in *mine arm, mine host,* which we still retain in poetry and in rhetorical use; but in the main *my* and *thy* were the forms for the attributive possessive, and *mine* and *thine* for the absolute possessive. The ending of *mine* and *thine* was imitated in *hern, hisn, ourn, yourn,* and *theirn* (some of which go back to the fourteenth century), but these forms survive only as vulgarisms. In educated English, however, the want of an 'absolute' possessive has been supplied, except in the case of *his,* by tacking on the ending of possessive nouns to the ordinary possessive pronoun. We say 'this house is *yours,*' just as we say 'this house is *John's.*' Perhaps it would have been better if the literary language had accepted *hisn,* but from some cause it did not do so.

It cannot be said that the prevalence of the French language in England down to the fourteenth century has left many traces in modern English grammar. We get from French the so-called feminine ending *-ess,* which we now add quite freely to native English words; but this does not strictly belong to grammar, any more than does our adoption of many other foreign suffixes, such as *-ment* and *-ize.* However, as the adoption of *-ess* has been mentioned, we may call attention to the curious fact that this ending has never been used in English for what one might have thought its most natural purpose, the formation of names of female animals. The few words that we have of this kind, like *tigress, lioness,* are not of English origin, but were adopted from Old French. In spite of the analogy of these substantives, it seems always to have been felt that the ending was appropriate only to designations of persons.

Probably it is in some degree owing to French influence that our langugae was able to develop one useful piece of grammatical machinery—namely, an additional mode of expressing the notion of the genitive case. We can still say 'David's son,' as our ancestors a thousand years ago said *Dauídes sunu* (or, less frequently, *se sunu Dauídes*); but we can also express the same meaning by saying 'the son of David,' which corresponds to the French *le fils de David*. In Old English *of* was mainly used where we should now use 'from' or 'out of.' The same sense also belongs to the French *de*. There are in Old English a few special instances in which *of* has a genitival sense (as in *se cyning of Norwegan*, the king of Norway), but the use of the preposition as a regular sign of the genitive first appears in the twelfth century. We do not know whether, apart from French influence, the English language would not have evolved this convenient device for obviating the ambiguities arising from the decay of the old inflexions; but imitation of French idiom certainly helped it to attain general currency. The many nouns adopted from French naturally formed their genitive after the French pattern; and the new form was also applied to those nouns which had lost their distinctive genitive inflexions. Ultimately it came to be admissible in the case of all substantives. If the inflected genitive had been driven out of use by the 'phrasal' genitive the result would have been a weakening of the language—a distinct loss of condensation and energy. Fortunately this did not happen; the form in *-s* was retained, but its use was restricted to instances in which it was convenient that the genitive should precede the governing noun instead of following it. In this way there was developed a difference in meaning and emphasis between the inflected and the phrasal genitive, and the fact that modern English possesses both enables us to express shades of meaning which cannot be rendered with equal precision either in French or Latin. For example, if we substitute the expression 'England's history' for the more usual 'the history of England,' we indicate that the name of the country is used with some approach to personification. Even where the signification of the two forms is identical, there is a distinction of emphasis or feeling which it is not easy for a foreigner to apprehend.

The rule that the genitive in *'s* must be followed immediately (or only with the intervention of an adjective, or an adjective qualified by an adverb) by the governing substantive, has given rise in modern English to the practice of treating the *'s* virtually as a separable word (a 'postposition,' as we might call it), and attaching it to a whole descriptive phrase expressing a single idea, as in 'the Duke of Devonshire's estates.' Colloquially, this practice is sometimes carried to quite grotesque extremes. We hear occasionally such sentences as 'That was the man I met at Birmingham's idea.' Here the intonation of oral speech, which cannot be reproduced in writing, shows that the phrase 'the-man-I-met-at-Birmingham' is for the nonce converted into a word, which can take the inflexional *'s* like any ordinary substantive. The 'group-genitive,' as it is called, is a useful addition to the resources of the language, as it is more direct and forcible than the synonymous form with *of*. The need for a 'group-plural' formed in a similar way, is sometimes felt. Such a formation is, for obvious reasons, inadmissible in writing, except in such simple cases as 'the Miss Smiths,' 'the two Dr. Johnsons,' but in conversation it would be possible, without causing much surprise, to speak

of 'a whole gallery of John the Baptists,' or (referring to
tavern signs) of 'the innumerable King's Armses and Duke
of Wellingtons.'

A grammatical innovation, of somewhat questionable
value, which is due to French influence, is the polite substitution of the plural for the singular in the second person.
The origin of this custom is to be found in the official Latin
of the later Roman Empire, in which a great person of state
was addressed with 'you' instead of 'thou,' just as, in formal
documents, he wrote 'we' instead of 'I.' The use of the
plural 'you,' as a mark of respect, passed into all the
Romanic languages, and from them into German, Dutch,
and Scandinavian. It is a well-known fact that forms of
politeness originally used only in addressing superiors have
in all languages a tendency to become more and more widely
applied; and hence in Europe generally the singular 'thou'
has, except in religious language and in diction more or less
poetical, come to be used only in speaking to intimate
friends or inferiors. In England, during the last two centuries, the use of *thou,* so far as ordinary language is concerned, has become obsolete; it is only among the speakers
of certain local dialects that it continues to be employed
even by parents to their children, or by brothers and sisters
to each other. Our language has thus lost whatever advantage it had gained by having a polite as well as a familiar
form of address; and unfortunately the form that has survived is ambiguous. There is a translation of the New
Testament into modern English in which *you* is everywhere
substituted for *thou,* except in addresses to the Deity. It is
a significant fact that in one place the translator has felt
obliged to inform his readers by a footnote that in the original the pronoun changes from the plural to the singular.
The English language is, in respect of clearness, decidedly

the worse for the change which has abolished the formal distinction of number in the second person of the pronoun and the verb.

One highly important feature of English grammar which has been developed since Old English days is what has been called the attributive use of the substantive, which may be exemplified by such expressions as 'a silk hat,' 'the London County Council,' 'the Shakspere Tercentenary,' 'Church of England principles,' 'a House of Commons debate,' 'the Marriage Law Amendment Act,' 'the half-past two train,' 'the London, Brighton, and South Coast Railway,' 'the Highstreet front of the Town Hall,' 'my lawyer cousin.' No other European language has anything exactly parallel to this usage. In German, it is true, many of the English attributive combinations could be rendered by compound nouns, which in that language may be formed very freely; but others must be translated by substituting an adjective for the attributive noun, and others again by a circumlocution of some kind. The difference between one of these English expressions and the German compound which corresponds to it is not merely that the latter is written as one word and the former is written with spaces between its parts. In speaking English we feel that the elements of such a combination are as much distinct words as are the adjective and the following substantive, or the genitive noun and the noun which governs it. The English noun used attributively might be described grammatically in various ways. We might say that the noun was in a *case* expressing a relation somewhat similar to that expressed by the genitive, but wider. Or we might say that it was a new part of speech, halfway between the substantive and the adjective. As English adjectives have no inflexions, there is no formal criterion by which we can distinguish an attributive substantive from an adjective; and in fact many substantives, from being often used attributively, come to be really adjectives. The germ from which the attributive use of substantives has been developed is the compound noun. In Old English, as in German, Greek, and other languages, two substantives could be put together to form one word. The accent of the word was placed on the first element, which served to limit the sense of the second element to a special application. English has still many compounds of this sort, such as *boókcase, coách-house, wáterpot;* and indeed we can form new words of this kind very freely. Now very often it happens that the first element of such a combination has (as used in this position) a sense in which it is nearly equivalent to an adjective or to a noun in the genitive. In such cases the two elements of a compound came in Middle English[9] to be apprehended as separate words, and each of them was pronounced with its independent accent. In this way it was that English grammar was enriched by the creation of the attributive noun. It often makes a noteworthy difference to the sense whether an attributive combination is taken as two words or as one. If we hear of 'the school-house' we think of a house which is used as a school; on the other hand, 'the school house' (with two accents) suggests a house which belongs to the school. The development of the attributive construction has greatly increased the flexibility and compactness of the language. As will

[9] It is difficult to fix the period at which this development began; it would be a great mistake to suppose that when a combination of substantives is in Middle English written as two words that affords any proof that the two were not apprehended as forming a compound. In Middle English, as in Old English, a genuine compound was very often written with the parts separated.

be seen from some of the examples given above, we can use a whole complex phrase attributively as if it were a single substantive.

Yet another means by which English has added to its resources of expression during the last thousand years is the extended use of auxiliaries in the conjugation of the verb. The Old English verb was very deficient in contrivances for indicating distinctions of tense. It had only two regular tenses, a present, which served also as future, and a past. A beginning had, however, been made towards supplementing this inadequate system by using certain verbs as auxiliaries, though these were employed only when the need for precise expression was especially urgent. If it was necessary unambiguously to designate an event as future, recourse was had to a figure of speech, much in the same way as a person who did not know how to form the future tense in some foreign tongue might say 'the sun is in debt to rise at six,' or 'coal intends to be cheaper.' The verbs which in Old English expressed the notion of debt or obligation and that of wish or intention were respectively *sceal* (our 'shall') and *wile* ('will'); and the figurative use of these verbs resulted in their being employed as mere signs of the future tense. When it was desired to express, more definitely than could be done by the simple past tense, the sense of what we call the perfect[10] or the pluperfect, the device employed was that of combining the present or past of the verb 'to have' with the passive participle.

---

[10] The use of the perfect tense is to indicate that a fact relating to the past is viewed as an element in the *present* condition or character of the subject, or as a portion of a history that extends to the present moment. Thus we can say 'England *has had* many able rulers,' but if we substitute 'Assyria' for 'England' the tense must be changed. It is allowable to say 'Aristotle *has treated* this subject in his *Ethics*,' just as we say 'Aristotle *says* so and so'; but we cannot say 'Aristotle has written the *Ethics*.'

It is easy to see how this contrivance was suggested. If I say 'I have a letter written,' where *have* is used in its primary sense, the sentence expresses the same fact as 'I have written a letter,' though it expresses something else in addition, viz., that the letter is still in my possession. From being used in cases of this kind, the combination of *have* with a participle naturally came to serve as a mere compound tense, as in 'he hæfth anne man *ofslægenne*,' literally, 'he has a man killed.' Here the participle agrees like an adjective with the object noun, but in later Old English it was made indeclinable. The practice of putting the object after the participle did not become general till the fourteenth century.

The perfect and pluperfect of intransitive verbs could be expressed in Old English by the verb *to be* and the participle, as we still do in sentences like 'Babylon is fallen,' 'the work is finished.' The latter form is ambiguous in the modern language, but it was not so in Old English, because the present and past of the passive were expressed by the auxiliary *weorthan*, literally 'to become' (equivalent to the German *werden*), which in later English was unfortunately lost.

In these auxiliary verbs Old English possessed an instrument of expression which admitted of being greatly developed. It was only necessary to conjugate each auxiliary through all its simple and compound tenses to produce a system capable of rendering almost every shade of meaning which is conveyed by the verbal inflexions of any language. The actual development, however, was gradual and slow; the abundant material which lay ready to hand was brought into use by degrees, in response to the growing need for accuracy of expression which was produced by the increased use of the language for literary composition.

We have not space to discuss in detail the history of the English system of verbal conjugation, but some few of its more remarkable features may be briefly pointed out.

One point that is especially worthy of notice is that the development of the functions of the verbal forms, in the direction of increase of clearness, has continued till very recent times, many changes of great value having taken place during the last three centuries.

We may consider in the first place the development of the auxiliary uses of the verb *to be*. Although the form 'I am speaking' came into use very early in Middle English[11] (the corresponding form of the past tense having existed already in Old English), it was not till the seventeenth century was well advanced that it became the regular expression for the true present as distinguished from the present of habit. Such a sentence as 'thy mother and thy sisters *seek* thee' was normal English when the Bible was translated; nowadays, in natural prose speech, we can only say 'are seeking.' The analogous passive forms, as in 'the house is being built,' 'he was being taught to ride,' were hardly known till near the end of the eighteenth century, and long afterwards they were condemned by sticklers for grammatical correctness. Yet the innovation was clearly needed: the older mode of speech, as in 'the house is building,' or even the fuller form used in the seventeenth century, 'the house is a-building,' could not be employed in all contexts without inconvenience. In such expressions as 'I have been working hard,' 'it has often been said,' 'if you were to do such a thing,' we have instances of the manner in which, by following out the analogy of older forms,

[11] There are one or two examples of it in Old English writings: *e.g.* in Ælfric's translation of Joshua x. 25.

the language has found means for representing shades of signification which had previously no accurate expression.

Another auxiliary which has acquired its most important function in quite modern times is the verb *to do*. In Old English, it was already possible to say 'I do speak,' 'he did answer' instead of the simple 'I speak,' 'he answered.' But down to the seventeenth century there is no very clear difference in meaning between the two forms. When, for instance, we read in the King James Bible of 1611, 'and they did eat, and were all filled,' it is not easy to see any reason, except the very good one that it improves the rhythm of the sentence, why the verb should be 'did eat' and not 'ate.' The words *do* and *did*, however, like any other auxiliary, admitted of being pronounced with strong stress, so as to emphasize the tense or the affirmative character of the sentence, or to give to the statement an exclamatory tone which intensifies the sense of the verb. This emphatic use of the auxiliary is obviously valuable, and it has gained in force and clearness from the fact that (during the last three centuries) the unemphatic *do* and *did,* in affirmative sentences, have become obsolete. In negative and interrogative sentences, on the other hand, the compound tenses formed with *do* and *did* have since Shakspere's time quite superseded the simple present and past, except in the case of a very few verbs, such as *do, have,*[12] and *be*. We can no longer say, in plain prose, 'I went not away,' 'Heard

[12] With regard to this verb there has been developed a convenient distinction in usage which seems to be in danger of being lost. The use of the auxiliary *do* is correct English only when *have* expresses something occasional or habitual, not when the object is a permanent possession or attribute. It is permissible to say 'Do you have breakfast at eight?' or 'We do not have many visitors'; but not 'Does she have blue eyes?' or 'He did not have a good character.' Many American writers violate this rule, and the faulty use appears to be gaining ground in England.

you the voice?' The explanation of the change perhaps is that owing to the more frequent use of compound tenses it became unusual for the particle *not* or the subject of an interrogative sentence to follow any verb but an auxiliary, so that instances in which this occurred were apt to sound unnatural.

The history of *shall* and *will* is another illustration of the continuous struggle of language towards clearness of expression. Our future auxiliaries are not very well suited to their purpose, because their meaning, as we have already mentioned, includes something besides the idea of future time. Intrinsically, therefore, they are inferior to the colourless and unequivocal German auxiliary *werden*. When we wish to express simple futurity, we are obliged to choose between two forms, one of which implies obligation, and the other will or intention. For many centuries the language was feeling its way to a rule for the employment of these forms, such that their excess of meaning should occasion the smallest amount of ambiguity. It is only in recent times that the problem has been solved: as is well known, the English Bible often has *shall* where we now feel that *will* would be more appropriate. The present rule, though Scotchmen and Irishmen still find it difficult to master, rests on a very intelligible principle. Future events are divided into two classes, those which depend on the present volition of the speaker, and those which do not. In the former case we say 'I will,' and 'you or he shall'; in the latter case we say 'I shall,' and 'you or he will.' There are many exceptions, each with its own special reason; but in the main the rule is correct. Some ambiguity in the use of *will* still remains possible, because such a statement as 'he *will* do it' may either express mere futurity or may mean that the person is determined to act in the manner indicated. The sense of *shall,* however, has become nearly unequivocal, and perhaps we may say that the language has at length succeeded in making the best possible use of its inherited means of expressing future time.

Much more might be said respecting the gradual enrichment of the English verbal conjugation. Owing very largely to the developments of the last three centuries, modern English is able to render with perfect precision almost every distinction in thought which is expressed by the modification of the verb in any language. It may, however, be remarked that the increased precision of modern English, though it is a great gain for the purposes of matter-of-fact statement, is sometimes the reverse of an advantage for the language of emotion and contemplation. Hence we find that our poetry, and our higher literature in general, often returns to the less developed grammar of the Elizabethan age.

3. PROFIT AND LOSS.

In the foregoing pages we have described, and tried to account for, the more important of the changes in the grammatical structure of English that have taken place since the days of King Alfred. We have now to ask how far the results of these changes have been good, and how far they have been evil, in their influence on the efficiency of the language as an instrument of expression.

It has been maintained by some scholars that in the evolution of language everything happens for the best, and that English in particular has lost nothing, at least so far as its grammar is concerned, that would have been worth keeping. But this extreme optimistic view can hardly be sustained. There can be no doubt that in writing

modern English special care and ingenuity are often required to avoid falling into ambiguities. Every unprac-
tised writer of English frequently finds it necessary to alter
a sentence which accurately expresses his meaning, because
he perceives that the reader might for a moment be in
doubt whether a particular word should be taken as a
noun or a verb, or whether, if it is a verb, it is meant for
the infinitive or the present tense. And if we venture on
those inversions of the normal order of words which when
skilfully used contribute so much to force and beauty of
expression, we have further to take care that the subject
of the sentence is not mistaken for the object. Much of
our poetry is obscure on a first reading, not because the
diction is affected or allusive, but because the structure of
the language has compelled the poet to choose between the
claims of lucidity and those of emphasis or grace. There
are passages in many English poets which are puzzling even
to native readers, but which if rendered literally into Latin
or German would appear quite simple and straightforward.
Of course it is possible to write as lucidly in English as in
any other language; but in order to do so we must use
constant watchfulness, and must sometimes reject the most
obvious form of expression for one that is more artificial.
In colloquial English, again, there are some abbreviations
which sometimes occasion inconvenience by their doubt-
ful meaning: thus *he's* may be either 'he is' or 'he has' and
I'd may be either 'I had' or 'I would.' It is true that no
known language is so perfect as not to have its own liability
to ambiguity,[13] and in this respect Old English was already

---

[13] For instance, in Latin (partly on account of the impairment of its inflexional system through phonetic change) there is an extraordinary abundance of forms which, apart from their context, would admit of two or
more different interpretations.

greatly inferior to Greek or even to Latin. Still, when the fullest allowance is made for this fact, it remains unquestionable that the loss of the Old English inflexions has not been unattended with disadvantage.

On the other hand, modern English, viewed with reference to its grammar, has certain merits in which it is scarcely rivalled by any other tongue. We have already pointed out the great value of some of the additions which the language has made to its grammatical resources during the last thousand years. But it is not merely by the acquisition of new machinery that English has gained in efficiency as a means of expression. The disappearance of superfluous inflexions, and the reduction of those which remain to mere consonantal suffixes which in most instances do not add a syllable, have greatly increased the capacity of the language for vigorous condensation. There are very few languages in which it is possible, as it is in English, to write whole pages almost exclusively in words of one syllable. Of course we are not compelled to do this: our language is quite as capable as any other of the variety of rhythm which is imparted by the use of words of differing length. But we cannot read any of our modern poets without seeing how much of force and impressiveness is often gained by the absence of syllables which denote mere grammatical relations that are irrelevant to the intended emotional effect. In modern English the grammar does not, as it does in purely inflexional languages,[14] obtrude itself on the attention where it is not wanted.

---

[14] As a somewhat extreme instance, we may cite the Latin *duōrum bonōrum virōrum*, where the main portions of the words, *du-*, *bon-*, and *vir-*, are actually unaccented, the stress falling on the endings which tautologically express three times over the notion of the genitive plural.

While English has thus the peculiar advantage of a noiseless grammatical machinery, it has another advantage of an opposite kind in its power of emphasizing certain grammatical relations by placing the sentence-accent on the auxiliary. It is usually difficult to render in another language the precise effect of the stressed auxiliary in such phrases as 'I *did* live there,' or 'if he *should* do such a thing.' The extensive use which is made of variation in sentence-accent for expressing distinctions of meaning gives a large scope for that elliptic brevity which is so striking a characteristic of spoken English. One remarkable example of the national love of conciseness of speech is our habit of omitting the principal verb in compound tenses where it can be supplied by the hearer from what has gone before, as in 'Yes, I do,' 'it certainly will not.' By means of this idiom we can under certain circumstances substitute a monosyllable for any tense of any verb.

The 'making of English grammar' is now probably a finished process. While it is certain that the vocabulary of English will in future undergo great changes—while many new words will be formed or adopted, and many old words will disappear or change their meaning—there is reason for believing that the grammar will remain for centuries very nearly what it is now. The ground for this belief lies partly in the spread of education. Literary culture perhaps on the whole conduces to tolerance of certain kinds of innovation in vocabulary, but with regard to grammar its tendency is strongly conservative. Another reason is that simplification of accidence has nearly attained its utmost conceivable limit, and that the few further steps in this direction that remain possible would involve practical inconvenience. For instance, our irregular verbs and irregular plurals of nouns are, as we have seen, for the most part shorter or more easily pronounceable than the regular inflexions that might be substituted. Perhaps if the influence of education did not stand in the way, the language might lose the distinctive *s* of the third person singular of the present tense, which is dropped in some forms of vulgar speech; but as things are this is very unlikely to happen. We cannot assert that the evolution of new grammatical material—for instance, of new auxiliary verbs—is altogether impossible, but the modern conservative instinct would render the acceptance of such novelties very difficult. On the whole, it is probable that the history of English grammar will for a very long time have few changes to record later than the nineteenth century.

III

What English Owes
to Foreign Tongues

The changes in grammatical structure, which were the subject of the preceding chapters, are only a part of the changes by which Old English has been transformed into Modern English. The changes in vocabulary are equally important. Although we still use many of the old words—chiefly, it is true, very much altered in pronunciation and spelling—yet a very considerable proportion of them have become obsolete; and many thousands of new words have been introduced. Of those new words which have been formed in English itself we shall have to speak later; in the present chapter we shall treat of those which have been adopted from foreign languages.

The adoption of foreign words into the English language began before the English came to this island. The Germanic people, of which the Angles and Saxons formed part, had long before this event been in contact with the civilization of Rome; and several Latin words, denoting objects belonging to that civilization, or foreign articles of use or luxury, had already found their way into the language of all or many of the Germanic nations. The Latin *strata*, a paved road, survives in English as *street*, and in German as

Strasse. Other words of Latin origin, which were learnt by the English people while still dwelling on the continent, and which remain in the modern language, are *wine, butter, pepper, cheese, silk, copper, pound, inch, mile, mint* (from Latin *moneta,* money).

When the English were settled in Britain, they learned a few more Latin words from the Romanized people of the towns. The Latin *castra,* for instance, became, under the form *ceaster,* the Old English word for a Roman fortified town, and it survives in the place-name Chester, and in the ending of many other names such as Winchester, Doncaster, Leicester, and Exeter.

In the sixth and seventh centuries, the people of England were converted to Roman Christianity, and one of the results of their conversion was that they adopted a considerable number of Latin words, chiefly signifying things connected with religion or the services of the church. Among those which are still part of the language are *bishop, candle, creed, font, mass, monk, priest.* Altogether, there have been counted about four hundred Latin words which had become English before the Norman Conquest; but many of these were not at all in common use, and only a few of them survive in modern English.

It might, perhaps, be naturally expected that Old English would contain many words taken from the language of the Celtic Britons. The older books on English philology contain a long list of words supposed to be derived from this source. Modern investigation, however, has shown that the number of Celtic words which are found in English before the twelfth century is less than a dozen; and of these several (such as *drȳ,* a wizard, the same word as *druid, bratt,* a cloak, *luh,* an arm of the sea, a *lough*) appear from their form to have been learnt not from the Britons, but from the Irishmen who accompanied the missionaries from Iona to Northumbria; while *dūn*, a hill, a 'down,' though of Celtic origin, was probably brought by the English from the continent. Perhaps *binn*, a manger, and *dunn*, dun (-coloured) and one or two more words, may really have been adopted from the British language, but these are all the Old English words for which this origin is at all probable. It must be confessed that this result is somewhat puzzling, as there is evidence to prove that the British population was not entirely massacred or driven westward by the English conquerors. The physical characteristics of modern Englishmen in many parts of the country show that they must be partly descended from the pre-English inhabitants; and in Old English writings *wealh*, Welshman, was one of the ordinary words for 'slave.' It must be remarked, also, that the British names of rivers and of cities have in many cases been preserved to modern times. Still, however surprising the fact may be, it remains certain that the English language owes practically nothing to the language of the ancient Britons.

To the Danes and Northmen the English vocabulary owes a great deal. If we did not otherwise know that England had once been under Scandinavian rule, we might have inferred the fact from the presence in our language of many Danish words with what may be called political meanings, such as *law, outlaw, grith* (legal security), *hustings, wapentake, riding* (in 'the three Ridings of Yorkshire'—the Old Norse *thrithjūngr*, third part). The Old English word *eorl* (earl), which originally meant merely a man of noble birth, came to be used in its Scandinavian sense of ruler of a district. Other words of Scandinavian origin are *awe, call, crave, fellow, get, hit, husband, knife, leg, loft, loose, low, odd, root, same, scant, skin, scrap, take,*

Thursday, thrall, want, wrong. The word *cross* of course comes ultimately from Latin, but its form is due to the Northmen, who had learnt it from the Christians of Ireland.* Some of our common words, which existed in Old English, have been assimilated to the kindred Scandinavian synonyms: thus *sister* descends not from the Old English *sweostor,* but from the Old Norse *syster;* and the Middle English *yive* or *yeve* (which regularly represented the Old English *gifan*[1]) has been superseded by the form *give* (Old Norse, *gifa*). In the dialects of the North of England, of East Anglia, and of some of the midland counties, there are scores of words of Danish origin.

We have now seen how far the English language had been enriched from foreign tongues before the end of the eleventh century. After all, the amount of what it had gained in this way was not very great in comparison with the whole extent of its vocabulary. With all the Latin, Celtic, and Scandinavian words that it had acquired, the general character of the language in 1100 was essentially what it had been five centuries before.

The new conditions brought about by the Norman Conquest, however, opened the door for a far more abundant influx of foreign words. It was not only that the tongue of the new rulers, as we have already seen, came to be used by large numbers of Englishmen in the intercourse of daily life, so that much of its colloquial vocabulary was adopted into the native language. The knowledge of French

[1] The Old English *g* before *i* and *e* was pronounced as *y*, and is represented by *y* in Modern English.

* The word *cross* came into early English from Old Irish by way of Old Norse. Ulteriorly it came from *crūx, crūcis,* the Roman instrument of punishment upon which criminals were impaled. The Old English word was *rōd,* our *rood* as in *roodloft* and *roodscreen.* — Simeon Potter.

gave access to the rich literature of the continent; from the thirteenth to the fifteenth century a large portion of the literature of England consisted of translations of French romance, and the native poetry was powerfully influenced by French models. Under these circumstances it was natural that the English literary dialect should receive a large accession of French words, many of which gradually found their way into the vocabulary of familiar speech.

There was yet another way in which the Norman Conquest contributed to the transformation of English from a purely Germanic language to one with a mixed vocabulary. The higher literary culture of the foreign clergy, who under Norman and Angevin rule were introduced into the English monasteries, soon made itself felt in the extended use of Latin for works of history and theology. In process of time many Latin chronicles and books of devotion were translated into English, and the translators, writing for readers who were not altogether without learning, often found it easier to adopt words from the learned language than to render them by native equivalents.

It is important to understand that the French words which were brought into English represent two different dialects. The form of the French language which obtained currency in England as the immediate consequence of the Norman Conquest was the northern dialect—the speech of Normandy and Picardy. But with the accession of the Angevin dynasty in the middle of the twelfth century the dialect of Central France became the language of the court and of fashionable society. The two dialects differed considerably in pronunciation: for instance, Northern French had *k* where Central French had *ch,* and *ch* where Central French had *s;* in words of Germanic and Celtic etymology the original *w* remained unaltered, while in Central French it became *gu,* and ultimately *g;* and in many words where Northern French had *g* the Central dialect changed it to *j.* One consequence of the twofold character of the French spoken in England was that very often one and the same French word was adopted into English twice over, in two different forms and with meanings more or less different. Thus we have in modern English the words *catch, warden, launch, wage,* which came from Norman French, and alongside them we have *chase, guardian, lance, gage,* which represent the same words as pronounced in the French dialect afterwards introduced. In this way the dialectal diversities in the language of the conquerors have contributed to increase the copiousness of the English vocabulary. There are a few cases in which a word was at first made English in its Norman form, and afterwards assimilated to the pronunciation of Central French: thus 'charity' was *cariteth* in the English of about 1150, but a century later it appears as *charitee.* It may be mentioned as a curious fact, that while the spelling *gaol* is derived from Northern French, the word is always pronounced, and sometimes written *(jail)* with the *j* which is a mark of the Central dialect.

It is interesting and instructive to observe what kinds of objects or ideas are chiefly denoted by the words that came in from French during the two centuries that followed the Conquest. Readers of *Ivanhoe* will remember the acute remark which Scott puts into the mouth of Wamba the jester, that while the living animals—*ox, sheep, calf, swine, deer*—continued to bear their native names, the flesh of those animals as used for food was denoted by French words, *beef, mutton, veal, pork, bacon, venison.* The point of the thing is, of course, that the 'Saxon' serf had the care of the animals when alive, but when killed

they were eaten by his 'French' superiors. We may perhaps find a similar significance in the French origin of
*master, servant, butler, buttery, bottle, dinner, supper,
banquet.* It is only what we should have expected that we
find French words abundant among our terms relating to
law, government, and property. Examples are *court, assize,
judge, jury, justice, prison, gaol, parliament, bill, act,
council, tax, custom, royal, prince, county, city, mayor,
manor, chattel, money, rent,* all words that came in before
the end of the thirteenth century. The system of gradation
of titular rank was of continental origin, and the individual titles are mostly French, as *duke, marquis, viscount,
baron.* There is one notable exception; the foreign *count*
(Old French *conte*) was not adopted, because the native
earl had come to have nearly the same meaning; but it had
not been the English custom to give ladies titles corresponding to those of their lords, and hence for the wife of
an earl the French title *countess* had to be used. The Old
English word *cniht* (knight) kept its place, possibly because
it was shorter than the French synonym *chevalier.*

It was natural, too, that many of the terms relating to
military matters should be adopted from the tongue of the
conquerors. *War* itself is a Norman French word, and
among the other French words belonging to the same department which became English before the end of the
thirteenth century are *battle, assault, siege, standard, banner, gonfanon, arms, armour, harness, glaive, lance, arbalest,
hauberk, mangonel, fortress, tower.*

In industrial civilization the French-speaking strangers
were no doubt greatly superior to the native population,
and it is probably for this reason that nearly all the commonest designations of classes of tradesmen and artisans
are of French origin. The smith, the baker, the skinner,

and a few more, kept their Old English titles; but the butcher, the barber, the chandler, the carpenter, the cutler, the draper, the grocer, the mason, the tailor, are all called by French names. The shoemaker is an exception, but there was a time when he preferred to call himself a cordwainer or a corviser.

It is curious to note that all the current terms of family relationship outside the immediate circle of the household have been adopted from French. *Uncle, aunt, nephew, niece,* and *cousin,* very soon displaced their native equivalents. *Grandsire* and *Grandame,* which appear in the thirteenth century, are words taken directly from the French spoken in England. They do not appear to have been used on the Continent; and indeed the substitution of the respectful titles *sire* (the same word as *sir*) and *dame* for 'father' and 'mother' appears to have been peculiar to the French of England. In the fifteenth century the half-English *grandfather* and *grandmother* came into use; but it was not until the Elizabethan times that the use of the prefix was extended (in a manner unknown to French) by the formation of words like *grandson* and *granddaughter. Father-in-law, mother-in-law,* etc., are formed of English elements, but they are literal translations of Old French designations. The words *sire* and *dame* (now *dam*), which, as we have just seen, were originally applied to parents as terms of respect, have suffered a strange descent in dignity of use, being now employed (except for the poetic use of *sire*) only with reference to animals.

The only definite class of objects for which the native names have remained without any French mixture (so far as colloquial use is concerned) is that consisting of the external parts of the body. Even here there is one noteworthy exception. The French word *face,* which first appears as English late in the thirteenth century, found admission into the vocabulary of familiar speech, perhaps all the more readily because it was shorter or more easily pronounced than the native synonyms, *onlete, onsene,* and *wlite.*

The literary, as distinguished from the colloquial, adoption of French words, began in the twelfth century, and has continued down to the present time. The English writers of the thirteenth and fourteenth centuries were able to assume on the part of their readers at least a moderate acquaintance with literary French. Hence they felt themselves at liberty to introduce a French word whenever they pleased. The poets availed themselves of this liberty very freely; it was an easy resource for meeting the necessities of rhyme and metre, and especially the very exacting demands of the laws of alliterative verse. The innumerable words brought into the language in this way are naturally of the most varied character with regard to meaning. Many of them, which supplied no permanent need of the language, have long been obsolete, but the greater number still survive. The French importations by prose writers during this period are less abundant, and consist largely of terms of science and theology, in which the native language was poor.

The French literary vocabulary, from an early period, contained a very large proportion of learned words taken from Latin, with the endings dropped or altered in accordance with the habits of French pronunciation. Words of this kind, when adopted into English, served as a pattern after which Latin words could be anglicized. An English writer who introduced a Latin word into his composition usually gave it the same form in which it would have been adopted into French. It is therefore often difficult or impossible to determine whether an English word of Latin origin came into English immediately from Latin or through the medium of French. Even when we have proved that the word was used earlier in French than in English, the question is not settled, because it may have been independently borrowed in the two languages; indeed, it is certain that this often did happen.

The custom of adopting Latin words at secondhand—through French—paved the way to the extensive introduction of words directly from Latin. This is the reason why the Latin element is so very much larger in the English vocabulary than in that of any other Germanic language—German, Dutch, or Scandinavian. Germany and Holland have certainly not been less, but probably much more, devoted to classical scholarship than England has; but their languages were not, in their middle stages, saturated with French loan-words, and consequently they were led to find expression for new ideas by development of their native resources, instead of drawing on the stores of the Latin vocabulary.

The Latin element in modern English is so great that there would be no difficulty in writing hundreds of consecutive pages in which the proportion of words of native English and French etymology, excluding particles, pronouns, and auxiliary and substantive verbs, would not exceed five per cent of the whole.[2] What would be the result of an etymological census of all the words in a complete modern dictionary it is impossible to say, because the laborious and unprofitable task has never been performed;

[2] In this statement it is assumed that all the words of Latin origin which conform to the accepted rules for anglicizing Latin words are to be counted as Latin and not as French, even though as a matter of history they may have been adopted through French.

but it is probable that, if compounds and derivatives of English formation were left out of account, the words taken from Latin would far outnumber those from all other sources. And the Latin portion of the vocabulary is still constantly receiving additions. The greater part of modern English literature has been written by men who were classically educated, and for readers who were presumed to have more or less knowledge of Latin. Probably there are very few of our scholarly writers who are not responsible for the introduction of some new word of Latin derivation. It has come to be felt that the whole Latin vocabulary, or at least that portion of it which is represented in familiar classical passages, is potentially English, and when a new word is wanted it is often easier, and more in accordance with our literary habits, to anglicize a Latin word, or to form a compound from Latin elements, than to invent a native English compound or derivative which will answer the purpose. So much is this the case, that probably the authors of many of these coinages would be greatly surprised to learn that the words had never been used before, or even that they were not to be found in the ordinary dictionaries. And the classically-educated reader, when he meets with a word of Latin etymology which he at once recognises as a good and useful expression of a certain meaning, does not ordinarily note that he has not been accustomed to meet with it in English. Our literary vocabulary abounds with words which owe their mental effect not to any English traditions, but to the reader's knowledge of the Latin etymology. Sometimes, even, a word depends for its precise force on its suggestion of a particular classical passage. For example the adjective *esurient*, which literally means only 'hungry,' is often used with an implication which is intelligible only to readers who remember the *Graeculus esuriens* of Juvenal—the 'hungry Greekling' who will shrink from no task that will bring him a little money.

The English method of adopting Latin words is in some respects peculiar. While in French, as a general rule, Latin adjectives are adopted by simply dropping the inflexional ending of the accusative, there is in English a curious aversion to doing this except in the case of words having distinctly adjectival endings. In other cases we ordinarily append a suffix, ultimately of Latin origin, either *-ous, -al,* or *-an.* This practice began in French, but in English it has been extended much farther. The Latin *continuum, caelestem, erroneum,* which in French have become *continu, céleste, erroné,* are in English *continuous, celestial erroneous;* the Latin *veracem* becomes *veracious* (not *verace*); and *caeruleus* becomes *cerulean.* A Latin adjective anglicized, as substantives usually are, by merely leaving out the ending, would strike every one as un-English, unless it had one of the familiar endings of adjectives. In the anglicizing of Latin verbs, one usual mode is that of dropping the inflexions of the present indicative; but where the verb has a short root syllable this mostly results in the production of forms which somehow are felt to be unsatisfactory. If the verb *dīvĭdo* had not become English at an early period, no one would now think of adopting it in the form *divide.* In many instances of this kind we can fall back on the old practice of forming the English verb from the passive participle, as in *revise, direct, inspect, meditate, expedite;* but where the participle happens to end in *-ĭtus* this resource is not in accordance with modern custom. Hence the general statement that any Latin word may be adopted into English if it supplies a want is in practice limited by the fact that there are many verbs (such as *desĭpio,* for instance) which do not admit of being anglicized according to the recognised methods.*

The revival of Greek learning in Western Europe, the effects of which began to be felt in this country soon after the commencement of the sixteenth century, opened up a new source from which the English vocabulary could be enriched. Long before this time the language contained a certain number of Greek words, such as *geography, theology, logic,* which had come in through the medium of Latin. In most cases the immediate source was French; and nearly all these latinized Greek words had been adopted into all the literary languages of Europe. In the sixteenth and to a great extent in the seventeenth century Latin was still the ordinary vehicle of the literature of science and philosophy, and the new technical terms of Greek etymology were generally used in modern Latin before they found their way into the vernacular tongues. It therefore became a general European convention that when a new word was adopted from Greek into English or any other modern language, it must be treated as if it had passed through a Latin channel. The Greek *k, ai, ei, oi, ou, u,* were transliterated, after Latin example, by *c, æ, i, œ, u, y,* and the aspirated initial *r* by *rh.* In the main, these rules are still adhered to, though there are some exceptions among modern scientific words. Greek adjectives, it may be remarked, are usually anglicized, like Latin adjectives by the addition of the suffix *-ous, -an,* or *-al:* thus

---

* One important feature of borrowing from Latin is concerned with adjectives in *-able.* These are formed by adding this suffix not to the past participle but to the root of the infinitive. We must be careful to say *isolable,* and not *isolatable; demonstrable,* and not *demonstratable; educable* and not *educatable,* etc. Notice, however, that this principle does not apply when the verb has only two syllables. We say *creatable,* and not *creable; dictatable,* and not *dictable, translatable,* and not *translable,* etc.—Simeon Potter.

autonomos, diaphanēs, are represented by *autonomous, diaphanous.*

Although the study of Greek has been for centuries an essential part of the higher education of Englishmen, the language would not have contributed very greatly to the English vocabulary, if it had not happened to be peculiarly well fitted to supply the need for precise technical terms of science. It possesses an unlimited power of forming compound words, and it has also a singularly complete and regular system of suffixes, by means of which a whole group of derivatives of obvious and precise meaning can be produced from any verb or noun. Thus the verb *zētēo,* I inquire, has the derivatives, *zētēma,* an object of inquiry, *zētēsis,* the process of inquiry, *zētētēs,* an inquirer, *zētētikos,* able or disposed to inquire; and the meaning of all these words is obvious when that of the primary verb is known. In the hands of the long succession of thinkers which culminated in Plato and Aristotle, the capacities of the language for the expression of accurate distinctions had been cultivated to the highest point. In all the departments of science that were known to the ancient world, the Greek technical vocabulary is marvellous in its lucidity and precision. It is therefore not wonderful that the greater part of it has been adopted into all the modern European languages. So well adapted is the structure of the Greek language for the formation of scientific terms, that when a word is wanted to denote some conception peculiar to modern science, the most convenient way of obtaining it usually is to frame a new Greek compound or derivative, such as Aristotle himself might have framed if he had found it needful to express the meaning.

The wonderful development of the physical sciences during the last two hundred years has created a necessity for the invention of a multitude of new terms; and hence an etymological census of the words in our recent large dictionaries would show a surprisingly[3] great proportion of Greek derivatives—a proportion which is constantly increasing. In addition to the scientific terms the recently-coined words of Greek etymology include many names of processes or instruments of modern invention such as *photography, lithography, ophthalmoscope, stereotype, telephone, cinematograph*. It is to be noted that the modern scientific and technical words from this source are mostly of international currency. The custom of forming compounds from Greek elements prevails in all civilized countries of Europe and America, and if a useful term of this kind is introduced in any one country—whether in England, France, Germany, Holland, Italy, or Spain— it is usually adopted with great promptitude into the languages of all the rest.

Nearly all the words that English owes to the Greek language, indirectly as well as directly, were originally scientific or technical, though many of those of older date (adopted through mediæval Latin and French), such as *fancy, idea, ecstasy, pathos, sympathy,* have long taken their place in the popular vocabulary. Now and then, though not very often, a Greek word of other than technical character is employed in anglicized form in order to evoke in the reader's mind a recollection of its use by some classic author. The use of such a word as *apolaustic,* for example, implies that the writer who uses it is addressing readers who are able to understand an allusion to the *Ethics* of Aristotle. There are, too, a few Greek words, such as *kudos,*

[3] At least if our anticipations are based on knowledge of the etymological composition of the vocabulary of every-day speech, or even of that of ordinary literature.

nous, hubris, which have been adopted, without the customary latinization of form, in university slang, and have thence acquired a certain degree of general currency.

During the four centuries that have elapsed since 1500, the intercourse between England and the remoter nations of Europe has become more extensive and intimate than in earlier times, and the literatures of those nations, made accessible through the printing press, have come to be studied in this country. At the same time, the progress of discovery and colonization, in which England has borne so great a part, has made known to our countrymen the languages, customs, and products of the most distant regions of the earth. Hence it has come to pass that the modern English vocabulary includes words derived from every civilized language of Europe, and from innumerable languages of Asia, Africa, America, and Australia.

A great deal of history is enshrined in the many words that English has adopted from other tongues The presence in our dictionaries of such terms as *aria, basso, cantabile, da capo, fantasia, finale, gamut, intermezzo, legato, maestoso, oboe, opera, piano, pizzicato, prima donna, rallentando, staccato, tremolo,* and *aquatinta, busto, chiaroscuro, dado, facciata, fresco, graffito, impasto, intaglio, mezzotint, morbidezza, ovolo, rilievo, replica, studio, terra cotta* (to mention only a few of many) would be sufficient to inform us, if we did not know already, that the Italians have been our teachers in music and the fine arts. Less generally known are the obligations of English artistic culture to the Netherlands, which are shown by such words as *landscape, sketch, easel,* and *maulstick.* That the Dutch were once our masters in nautical matters may be learned from the terms *aloof, avast, boom, dock, hull, skipper, orlop, flyboat, euphroe, rover,* and many others. There was a period when the 'Englishman Italianate,' whom Ascham so much detested, was a personage very commonly met with, and when Italy set the fashion for England in literary taste as well as in dress and social customs; there was another period in which the Spaniards Gongora and Guevara were looked on as the writers most deserving of admiring imitation. It is therefore not wonderful that the English of the books written during these periods contains many words adopted from Italian and Spanish. Some of these did not take root in the language, but others are still in current use, as *attitude, cicerone, fiasco, influenza, isolate, motto, stanza, umbrella,* from Italian, and *ambuscade, desperado, disembogue, dispatch, grandee, negro, peccadillo, punctilio, renegade,* from Spanish. Amongst the very few words that English owes to High German are *bismuth, blende, cobalt, gneiss, greywacke, quartz, shale, zinc,* which remind us that it was in Germany that mineralogy first attained the rank of a science.

The English words taken from the other languages of Europe, and from languages of more distant parts of the world, are chiefly names of foreign products, or terms connected with the customs of foreign peoples. From Portuguese we have *auto-da-fe, albatross, cocoa, dodo, verandah;* from modern Greek, *valonia;* from Russian, *droshky, knout, verst, steppe;* from Turkish, *caftan, coffee, effendi, horde;* from modrn Scandinavian tongues, *eider, geyser, kraken, sloyd, tungsten.* The many languages of our Indian Empire are abundantly represented in our English dictionaries. The number of Malay words in English is surprisingly large, and though most of them are probably known to few people, the list includes the familiar *gingham, gong, gutta-percha, lory, orang-outan, amuck, ketchup.* China has given us *tea,* and the names of the various kinds of tea; a good many other Chinese words figure in our larger dictionaries, though they cannot be said to have become really English. From Japan, besides the terms relating to the art and the institutions of that country, we have *rickshaw,* which seems likely to become naturalized in an application unknown in its native land. The Polynesian dialects yield two words that are in everyday use, *taboo* and *tattoo.* The languages of the New World have contributed some hundreds of words; and although many of these, such as *squaw* and *wigwam,* are used only in speaking of the peoples to whose tongues they belong, there are not a few (e.g., *tobacco, potato, toboggan, moccasin, pemmican*) which we never think of regarding as foreign.

The increase of the English vocabulary by additions from foreign sources has been so enormous that the words of native etymology bear a very small proportion to the whole number of words given in our modern dictionaries. It is true that not a quarter of the words in the dictionaries are really familiar to the mass of well-educated readers. But even if we take the actual vocabulary of modern novels or newspaper articles, it still remains true that the words of Old English origin are far outnumbered by those derived from other tongues.

It has often been contended that the influx of foreign words into English has enfeebled instead of strengthening the language, and that it would have been better if, instead of taking over words from French and Latin, our countrymen had, like the Germans, supplied the need for new words by forming compounds and derivatives from the words belonging to the native stock. The advocates of this view have, no doubt, some facts on their side. It is a real defect in English that such words as *mind* and *mental,* *eye* and *ocular, sun* and *solar, moon* and *lunar, bone* and *ossify,* have no formal relation corresponding to their relation in meaning. And we shall see in a subsequent chapter (p. 85) that our language has suffered some injury in the partial loss of its capacity for forming compound words. On the whole, however, the effect of the etymological diversity of the vocabulary has been to provide the language with an unequalled profusion of approximate synonyms expressing subtle shades of difference in meaning and in tone of feeling. The distinction between such pairs of words as *paternal* and *fatherly, fraternity* and *brotherhood, celestial* and *heavenly, fortune* and *luck, felicity* and *happiness, royal* and *kingly,* is very real to an Englishman who knows his own language, but is not easy to render in any other tongue.

It is true, as a general rule, that when there are two words expressing approximately the same notion, one of them being of native and the other of French or Latin etymology, the native word is the one that has the fuller emphasis, and the greater richness of emotional suggestion. This fact, however, by no means justifies the rule which some writers have laid down and tried to carry out in practice, that 'Anglo-Saxon' words should be substituted for those of Latin etymology wherever it is possible to do so. Over-emphasis, force of diction in excess of the strength of the feeling that is to be rendered, is a falsity in style no less blameworthy than the opposite vice of inadequate expression. It must be remembered, also, that the peculiar depth of meaning of our native English words is largely due to the existence of the less vigorous synonyms of Latin origin, which enables us to reserve the nobler words for noble uses. If we accustom ourselves to use strong words where no emphasis is needed, and words fraught with beautiful suggestion when our matter is trivial, we shall be merely contributing to the debasement of our native language. The cry for 'Saxon English' sometimes means nothing more than a demand for plain and unaffected diction, and a condemnation of the idle taste for "words of learned length and thundering sound," which has prevailed at some periods of our literature. So far, it is worthy of all respect; but the pedantry that would bid us reject the word fittest for our purpose because it is not of native origin ought to be strenuously resisted.

It is not uncommon to meet with sneers at the pedantry of English men of science in framing their technical words from Greek and Latin, when they might express their meaning by words taken from the vocabulary of common life. There is no doubt that it is foolish to use technical terms when scientific precision is unnecessary, and where the meaning may be as well expressed in words intelligible to the unlearned. But, on the other hand, every science needs its special vocabulary of terms that can be definitely limited to one precise meaning. It would have been possible to construct a vocabulary for modern science consisting of popular words taken in arbitrarily restricted senses, and of compounds formed out of native English elements. In German, indeed, this kind of thing has been done to a very considerable extent. But it is often a positive disadvantage that a scientific word should suggest too obtrusively its etymological meaning. A term which is taken from a foreign language, or formed out of foreign elements, can be rigidly confined to the meaning expressed in its definition; a term of native formation cannot be so easily divested of misleading popular associations. If, for example, the English founders of the science of geology had chosen to call it 'earth-lore,' every one would have felt that the word ought to have a far wider meaning than that which was assigned to it. The Greek compound, which etymologically means just the same thing, has been without difficulty restricted to one only of the many possible applications of its literal sense. Sometimes also a scientific term embodies in its etymology a notion which the progress of discovery shows to have been erroneous or imperfect: thus the name *oxygen,* formed by the French chemists from Greek elements, literally implies that the element so called is the distinctive constituent of acids. If our chemists, instead of adopting the word as it stands, had framed a native compound of corresponding meaning (as the Germans have done in their *Sauerstoff*), the retention of the name would have had the inconvenient result of suggesting to beginners in chemistry an erroneous notion. As it is, we can continue to speak of 'oxygen' without thinking of its etymology, while if we do happen to know the literal sense we may learn from it an interesting fact in the history of science. There is some ground for the complaint that the student who is ignorant of Greek and Latin may find the existing terminology of modern science a severe burden on his memory. But this disadvantage, though real, is far smaller than those that would result from any thoroughgoing attempt to introduce vernacular equivalents for the terms of classical derivation. It is, however, much to be desired that men of science would take greater pains to fashion their new words in accordance with correct philological principles.

Against the sentimental purism that regards mixture in language as a sin which no gain in expressive power can atone for, it would be vain to attempt to argue. But if we are content to estimate the worth of a language by its efficiency in fulfilling the purposes for which language exists, we cannot reasonably deny that English has been immeasurably improved by its incorporation of alien elements. The slender vocabulary of Old English might, no doubt, have attained a great degree of copiousness purely by development of its native resources, without foreign aid; but, so far as we can see, the subtlety and varied force characteristic of modern English could never have been acquired by this means. It is true that our language is a difficult instrument to use with full effect, on account of its richness in those seeming synonyms which ignorant or careless writers employ without discrimination; but in skilled hands it is capable of a degree of precision and energy which can be equalled in few languages either ancient or modern.

IV

Word-Making in English

The English language has augmented its resources not only by the adoption of words from other tongues, but also by the making of new words. There are three possible ways in which a new word can be made: (1) by *Composition,* which means the joining together of two existing words to form a compound; (2) by *Derivation,* which means the making of a new word out of an old one, usually by the addition of some prefix or suffix which is not itself a word, but is significant in combination; and (3) by *Root-creation,* which is the invention of an entirely new word, usually either imitative of some inarticulate noise, or suggested by some instinctive feeling of expressiveness.

1. COMPOSITION.

A compound word is a word formed by joining two or more words to express a meaning that could be rendered by a phrase of which the simple words form part. Some languages have no compound words at all; and those which have them do not all form them after the same manner.

The principles of English word-compounding are, to a
great extent, inherited from the primitive Indo-Germanic
language. In those kinds of compounds that most frequently occur, the last element expresses a general meaning which the prefixed element renders less general. Thus
an *apple-tree* is a tree, but only a particular kind of tree.
In the original Indo-Germanic language the prefixed element in a compound of this sort was not, properly speaking, a *word*, but a word-stem: that is to say, a word deprived
of those grammatical characters—case, number, gender,
mood, tense, person, etc., which it would possess if it occurred separately in a sentence.[1] It has still this character,
so far as meaning is concerned, in those English compounds
that are formed on the inherited pattern. Thus *apple-* in
apple-tree is neither singular nor plural, neither nominative, accusative, nor genitive. Hence the phrase for which
such a compound is the condensed expression admits of
great variety of form; the former of the two words may
occur in it in any case or in either number; and the meaning of the compound varies accordingly. A *tree-frog* is a
frog that lives in trees; a *tree-fern* is a fern that is a tree;
a *tree-fruit* is the fruit produced by a tree. As a general
rule, our knowledge of the things denoted by the simple
words guides us at once to a correct understanding of the
meaning of the compound. This, however, is not always
the case. A *house-boat* might very well mean a sort of boat

---

[1] This comes out clearly in such a language as Greek, which has preserved
the primitive Indo-Germanic system of inflexions. Thus *oikodespotēs* is
Greek for 'master of a house'; but while *despotēs*, 'master,' is a real word,
oiko-, 'house,' is only a stem. To make it into a word, capable of being
used in a sentence, we must add the endings that mark case and number,
as in *oikos*, nom. sing., *oikon*, acc. sing., *oikou*, gen. sing., *oikoi*, nom. pl.,
oikous, acc. plural.

usually kept in a boat-house, or a boat that belongs to a house, or that supplies the needs of houses. It is only custom that has decided that the compound word shall mean a boat that serves as a house. The general meaning of this class of compounds might be expressed by saying that the noun which is formed of the two nouns A and B means 'a B which has some sort of relation to an A or to A's in general.'

The compounds formed by prefixing one noun to another, however, constitute only one out of the many classes of compounds which exist in English. There are compounds of adjective and noun, as *blackbird, hotbed;* of adverb and noun, as *downfall;* of noun and adjective, as *grass-green, purse-proud, penny-wise;* of adjective or adverb and adjective, as *dark-blue, ever-young;* and of noun or adjective and verb, as *wiredraw, whitewash;* and the very many compounds of adverb and verb, such as *overcome, inlay, outlive, upturn.* In all these cases the literal meaning of the compound is that of the last element, only limited or specialized. There are other compounds to which this description is not applicable. We have, for instance, adjectives like *barefoot* (having the feet bare); nouns like *redstart* (a bird which has a red 'start' or tail); and adjectives like *long-haired, five-leaved, lion-hearted,* which are derivatives formed from combinations of two words. From the fifteenth century onwards many compound nouns and adjectives have been formed in imitation of French, in which the first element is a verb-stem (in the original examples it was the imperative of a verb) and the second element is a noun denoting the object of the action, as in *breakfast, breakneck, kill-joy, makeshift, save-all, scapegrace, scarecrow, spendthrift, tosspot, turnkey.* We have also many nouns and adjectives compounded with a verb-stem and an adverb, as *break-up, come-down, knock-out, run-away.*

Some of the types of compounds enumerated above are formed on patterns which have come down by tradition from times before the English or even the Germanic language had any existence, when the elements that were joined in composition were not words but mere word-stems; while others were originally what are called by grammarians 'improper' or 'spurious' compounds. An improper compound is a phrase consisting of words in regular syntactical relation, which has come to be regarded as a single word. Such, in modern English, are *father-in-law, man-of-war, jews'-harp.* Words like *tradesman* and *gownsman* may be regarded as improper compounds, because they are at any rate imitated from phrases in which the first word was a noun in the genitive case.

From the point of view of the modern language, in which the loss of inflexions has obscured the difference between words and word-stems, and in which the attributive use of the noun is an ordinary part of syntax, the distinction of 'proper' and 'improper' compounds is only partially valid; but historically it is of considerable importance.

As any page of an 'Anglo-Saxon' dictionary will show, compound words were abundant in Old English; and in every succeeding age of the language a multitude of new compounds have come into existence. And yet, if we take a page of modern German and place beside it a good translation into English, we shall not fail to perceive that the compound words are very much more numerous in the German original than in the English rendering. Another noteworthy fact is that a great number of compounds, once generally used, are now obsolete, although the simple words composing them are still universally familiar. It may be worth while to inquire why this has happened.

Although word-composition, in those languages which freely admit it, is one of the readiest means of supplying the need for new words, compounds are often somewhat awkward in actual use. A compound word is a description, often an imperfect description; and when an object of perception or thought is familiar to us, we desire that its name shall suggest the thing to our minds directly, and not through the intervention of irrelevant ideas. Accordingly, a compound word for a simple notion gives a certain sense of inconvenience, unless we are able to forget its literal meaning. It is true that we frequently succeed in doing this: we use multitudes of compound words without mentally analysing them at all. In such cases the compound often undergoes processes of phonetic change which a distinct consciousness of its etymological meaning would not have allowed to take place. Thus the Old English *gōdspel,* literally 'good tidings' (which early became *gŏdspel,* through misreading the first element as 'God' instead of 'good'), is now *gospel;* the late Old English *hūsbonda,* a compound of *hūs* house and *bonda* dweller, cultivator, is now not *housebond* but *husband;* the poetical designation *day's eye* is now *daisy,* a word which we never think of as containing two elements; *holy day* has become *holiday;* *Christ's mass* is now *Christmas,* with an altered pronunciation which quite disguises the first word. This process is especially observable in place-names, where, even more than in ordinary compound words, the original descriptive meaning is a palpable irrelevance. Very few names of English places are now intelligible to persons unlearned in etymology, even when the separate words of which they are composed are still familiar in everyday speech. The Old English *stān* survives as 'stone,' and *tūn* as 'town'; but the place-name *Stāntūn* is now not 'Stonetown' but 'Stanton.' *Pedridan-tūn,* the 'town' or farm enclosure on the river Pedride, is now Petherton, though the name of the river has come to be pronounced 'Parret.'

A consideration of these and similar examples will show that compound words have often the disadvantage that their etymological meaning has to be forgotten before they can become quite satisfactory instruments of expression. It would appear that the English are, from whatever cause, more conscious of this inconvenience than are the speakers of some other languages. At any rate, although many new compounds have been formed in every period of the language, a large proportion of them have been short-lived or of very limited currency: the general tendency has been to replace them by other words. In the Middle English period this tendency was fostered by the circumstance that the two fashionable languages, French and Latin, make very little use of composition; and the common practice of adopting words from these languages made it easy to find substitutes for the native compounds. The Old English names for arts and sciences—such as *lǣcecrǣft* (leechcraft) for medicine, *scopcrǣft* for poetry, *tungolcrǣft* for astronomy, *rīmcrǣft* for arithmetic—disappeared early from the language, their places being taken by words adopted through French from Latin, or through French and Latin from Greek. The fourteenth century monk who wrote *ayenbite* (*of inwyt*) for 'remorse (of conscience)' did not succeed in inducing any other writer to use his new word: the Latin-French synonym was felt to be better for its purpose. Even now, a well-established compound is often partly superseded by a simple word or a derivative: for example, we use the word *steamer* more frequently than *steamboat* or *steamship*.

The habit of freely adopting foreign words, which has been produced by the conditions under which the English language has been developed, has had the good effect of relieving us from the necessity of having recourse to composition in cases where a compound, as such, is less suitable for our purpose than a simple word. But, on the other hand, our language has lost something of its capacity for forming compounds even where they would be useful. When Carlyle, imitating the German *Schadenfreude,* speaks of "a mischief-joy, which is often a justice-joy," we somehow feel that these formations are alien to the genius of the language, though if it were not for this the words would have been welcome additions to our vocabulary. It would seem un-English to say that a person was *rank-proud,* though the apparently analogous *purse-proud* has long been a recognised word; and *country-love* or *virtue-love* for 'love of country,' 'love of virtue,' would be equally inadmissible. And yet not only does modern English possess an enormous number of compounds, but new ones are continually introduced; and, what is still more remarkable, many of these additions to our language, when we first hear them, do not seem in the slightest degree novel. Probably nobody has ever used or ever will use the word *purple-eared;* but if the meaning ever needs to be expressed no one will say that the word is not English. It is not easy to say definitely what kinds of compounds are rejected by the instinct of the language and what kinds are freely admitted. In general, the new compounds that find ready acceptance are those which belong to some particular type or pattern which is exemplified in a large number of common words. One such type is that of the so-called 'parasynthetic' formation, like *blue-eyed, long-haired, swallow-tailed*. English idiom leaves us almost as free to invent new compounds of the type of *blue-eyed* as to invent new phrases of the type of *with blue eyes*. When one or both the elements happen to be very commonly used in combinations of this kind, the compound adjective, whether we have met with it before or not, is quite as natural a mode of expression as the equivalent phrase. But when this is not the case, the 'parasynthetic' adjective, though still allowable, strikes us as somewhat artificial, and a composition in which such words occur very frequently is apt to sound affected.

There are several other types of composition which are so familiar to us from the multitude of existing specimens that we can employ them almost without restriction to form new words. For instance, we seldom hesitate to make, whenever we feel the need of it, a new compound on the pattern of *coach-house, hair-brush, water-jug,* where the first element indicates the particular use to which the object designated is adapted. It may be remarked that the composition of long polysyllables is generally avoided as ungraceful: and, further, that most of the words derived from French and Latin appear somewhat unfrequently in compounds, probably because in the periods when word-composition was most frequent they were still felt to be more or less exotic.

With reference to the formation of compound verbs, modern English is somewhat peculiar in its usages. Perhaps the reader may be familiar with the practice of modern German in dealing with what are called separable prefixes.

In the German dictionaries we find a verb *aufgeben,* compounded of the adverb *auf* 'up' and the verb *geben* 'to give.' In the infinitive this is written as one word, the adverbial part coming first. So it is, under certain conditions, in the indicative and subjunctive; but 'I give it up' is ordinarily rendered in German by *ich gebe es auf,* where the two elements are treated as separate words, the adverb coming last, with the object-pronoun between it and the verb. Now combinations of this sort may, from one point of view, be regarded as phrases rather than as compounds; the adverb and the verb are really separate words. The idiom of the language requires that under some conditions the adverb shall precede the verb and that under other conditions it shall follow it; and in the former case custom has ordered that the two words shall be written as one. In Old English the position of the adverb was similarly variable (though the rules for its position were not so strict as in German); but in modern English prose we must always put the adverb last. In poetry, indeed, there are exceptions. Browning writes:

> "Then a beam of fun *outbroke*
> On the bearded mouth that spoke."

But *outbroke* is merely poetical: in plain prose we must say 'broke out.' We can, if we please, call *give up, break out, set up, put through,* and such like, 'compound verbs'; and in a certain sense the appellation is quite justifiable. If we adopt this nomenclature the number of compound verbs in English is beyond all calculation, and in fact we are continually inventing new ones. In its power of expressing fine distinctions of meaning by this method English vies with Greek and German, and has a great advantage over the Romanic languages, which have hardly any compound verbs at all.

But alongside these 'virtual compounds,' English has a considerable number of verbs formed with prefixed adverbs, such as *overtake, upset, understand*. In most cases their meaning is not obvious from their composition, and it is usually quite different from that of the combination of the verb with the following adverb. 'To overtake a person' does not mean the same as 'to take a person over'; 'to upset a thing' happens to have a meaning quite opposite to that of 'to set a thing up.' Compounds of this class originated in an older stage of the language: the principle of composition which they represent has almost died out, so that as a rule we cannot form any new words on the same pattern. We can, it is true, with some degree of freedom, prefix *over* and *under*, with the sense 'too much,' 'too little,' to verbs; but in general the modern feeling of the language resists the introduction of compounds of this kind, and very few of them have come in since the sixteenth century.

It is equally foreign to the spirit of the modern language to add to the number of those compound nouns or adjectives which are formed by prefixing an adverb to a verb-stem, a verbal noun, or a participle, such as *outbreak, outfit, income, downfall, downsitting, uprising, onlooker, outfit, forthcoming, downtrodden*. The method of formation of these words is a relic of the time when in a verbal phrase the adverb could precede the verb—when, for instance, it was as natural to say 'to out break' as 'to break out'; but new compounds of the kind could be easily formed down to the seventeenth century. They are fairly abundant, and admirably expressive; but we have almost[2]

---

[2] A word of this formation which has recently [late nineteenth century] gained some currency in journalistic use is *upkeep*, meaning '(cost of) keeping up.' It appears to have been imported from the Scottish dialect, in which this mode of composition has been more generally used than in standard English. From the same source we have obtained *outcome* (brought into literary English by Carlyle) and *uptake*.

entirely ceased to form new words on the same pattern. Although we perhaps more frequently say 'to fit up' than 'to fit out,' it would seem very eccentric to speak of an *upfit,* or an *upfitter;* and we should not think of using *downbroken* as a parallel to *downtrodden.* Cyclists talk of 'lighting-up time,' not of 'uplighting time,' which would be quite unidiomatic. Indeed many such compounds that were once current are now gone out of general use. The translators of the King James Bible could write 'My down-sitting and mine uprising'; but in natural modern English the equivalent expression would be 'my sitting down and my rising up.' Not long ago a very able foreign scholar, writing a grammatical treatise in English, puzzled his readers by using the word *down-toners* as a name for the class of adverbs which (like *rather, somewhat*) 'tone down' the force of the words to which they are prefixed. No doubt, if the phrase 'to tone down' had existed in the sixteenth century, a writer of that period could have spoken of a 'down-toner' without any risk of not being understood. But in this respect the language has undergone a change, which may be a change for the worse but which it would be vain to try to resist.

The composition of an agent-noun with a *following* adverb, which was foreign to English in its earliest stages, has been fairly common from the fourteenth century onwards. Chaucer has "*holdere up* of Troye"; Lydgate speaks of Nimrod as "*fynder up* of false religions"; Shakspere has "the *finder-out* of this secret"; the Bible of 1611 has "a *setter-forth* of strange gods"; later examples of this mode of formation are *cutter-out, hanger-on, filler-in, fitter-up.*

The English of poetry and of impassioned writing differs considerably in its principles of word-composition from the English of ordinary prose. Most of the compounds that are in ordinary use are too lifeless, too unsuggestive, or too trivial in association to be freely employed in poetry, while, on the other hand, our poets have generally assumed great liberty in the invention of compounds which in prose would be quite inadmissible. In this respect, however, there are great differences between poets, even those who are most nearly equal in rank. While Shakspere abounds with splendid audacities such as *"proud-pied* April," "a *heaven-kissing* hill," "the *world-without-end* hour," Spenser's inventions of this kind are comparatively few, though the exceeding felicity of some of them (as *"self-consuming* care," *"silver-dropping* tears") causes them to make an impression that has led many to suppose that they are peculiarly characteristic of his style. *"Rosy-fingered* Morn," which occurs in Spenser, is a literal rendering of Homer's *rhododaktulos Ēōs.* The translators of Homer, from Chapman downwards, have naturally been led to imitate the compound epithets of the original; and, partly through this channel, and partly owing to the classical learning of our poets, the copious word-composition of Greek has had great influence on the diction of English poetry. Of the greater poets of the nineteenth century, Wordsworth is the most sparing in the use of compounds, and this characteristic may be accounted for by his love of simplicity and naturalness of expression, and his aversion to the production of poetic effect by any other means than the direct appeal of thought and feeling to the mind of the reader. There is generally little in common between Wordsworth and Byron; yet Byron's rhetorical fervour is little more favourable to the use of this means of expression than is the simplicity of the other poet. He employs but few compounds, and hardly ever any that were not already current. On the other hand, Shelley, Keats, Tennyson, and Browning are all, for different reasons founded in their diversities of poetic temperament, remarkable for their fertility in the invention of novel compounds. It would be highly interesting to consider how the differences of spirit and feeling in these poets reveal themselves in the different ways in which they employ this method of enriching their vocabulary; but the matter belongs rather to the domain of the literary critic than to that of the student of language.

2. DERIVATION.

Old English was considerably less rich than Modern English in methods of making new words by derivation. It is true that a large portion of the Old English vocabulary consists of words derived from other words that existed in the language. But very many of these derivatives had been already formed before the English came over from the continent, and the processes by which they were made had become obsolete before the date of the earliest Old English literature. Perhaps this statement may need a little illustration to make it clear to readers unacquainted with philology. Everybody can see that the word *laughter* is derived from the verb *laugh;* and yet we should never think of forming a new substantive by the same process from any other verb. One of Mr. F. R. Stockton's personages, indeed, speaks of a dog "bursting into *barkter*," but nobody would seriously propose to coin a new word of this kind. The ending *-ter* is no longer 'a living suffix,' and, in fact, it had ceased to be such before Old English existed as a separate language. Many other suffixes which appear in Old English derivatives were, in like manner, never used in the formation of new words.

There is in English a large class of derivative verbs which, if there were no other evidence but that afforded by Old English itself, we should have to regard as formed from other Old English words, either nouns, adjectives, or verbs, by altering their vowel. Thus we find a noun *talu*, tale (in both senses, 'number' and 'story') and a verb *tellan*, to tell (again in both senses, 'to count' and 'to narrate'); a noun *salu*, sale, and a verb *sellan*, to sell. *Tȳnan*, to enclose, is derived from *tūn*, enclosure; *blēdan*, to bleed, from *blōd*, blood; *blǣcan*, to bleach, from *blāc*, white or pale; *fiellan*, to fell, cause to fall, from *feallan* to fall. A comparison of these words with their equivalents in the other Germanic languages teaches us that the true account of their origin is as follows: By the addition of a suffix *-jo* (pronounced *yo*) to the stem of the substantive, adjective or verb a new verb-stem was formed, to which the endings of mood, tense, and person were appended. The earlier forms of the verbs above mentioned were *taljan, saljan, tūnjan, blōdjan, blaikjan, falljan*. In prehistoric Old English the *j* in this position always produced an alteration in the vowel of the preceding syllable (unless that vowel was *ĭ*, *ī*, or *ǣ* and caused the preceding consonant to be lengthened or doubled if the vowel before it was short). Hence *taljan* became first *telljan* and then *tellan*, *blōdjan* became *blēdan;* and so with the rest. But all this had already taken place before Old English became a written language; and when it had taken place there was an end to the possibility of forming any new 'verbs of making or causing' by the process which had previously been so easy. All the verbs apparently formed by vowel change that existed in Old English were inherited from prehistoric times. Perhaps we might have expected that new derivatives would have been formed by vowel-change, in imitation of those which already existed (for instance, a verb *gēdan*, to make good, might have been formed from *gōd*, imitating the relation between *cōl* cool and *cēlan* to cool); but, so far as we know, nothing of the sort ever happened. The Old English language, at the earliest period at which it is known to us, had already lost one of the most useful of the means for word-making which it originally possessed.

Almost all those modes of derivation which were actually current in Old English have continued in constant use down to the present time. Only a few of the most important of them need be mentioned here. In Old English, a verb could be formed from a noun by attaching the conjugational endings to the stem of the noun: thus, from *wilcuma*, a welcome guest, was formed the verb *wilcumian* to welcome (*ic wilcumige* I welcome, *ic wilcumode* I welcomed). In later English, through the dropping away of final syllables, the infinitive, the imperative, and the plural and the first person singular of the present indicative of the derived verb have the same form as the primary noun, so that what takes place seems to be not the making of a new word but the using of a noun as a verb. Hence the operation has become, in modern English, so easy that we perform it almost unconsciously. In colloquial language, we can make new verbs with extraordinary freedom, not only from nouns, but even from phrases. "He 'my-dear-fellow'-ed me all the day," for instance, is quite permissible conversational English. Conversely, in modern English, we have an almost unlimited number of nouns which are merely verbs used substantively to denote an act. We can speak of 'a wash,' 'a shave,' 'a think,' 'a tumble down,' 'a dig in the ribs.' Occasionally it happens that a noun in this way gives rise to a verb, which in its turn gives rise to another noun, all three words being exactly alike in sound and spelling. Thus, in the following examples: (1) 'The *smoke* of a pipe,' (2) 'To *smoke* a pipe,' (3) 'To have a *smoke*,' the noun of (1) is not, strictly speaking, the same word as the noun of (3). It is true that in cases like this our dictionaries usually treat the secondary noun as merely a special sense of the primary noun; and, indeed, very often this treatment is unavoidable, because the difference of meaning between the two is so slight that in some contexts it disappears altogether. Still, it ought not to be forgotten that from the historical point of view the two nouns are really distinct: if English had retained its original grammatical system this would probably have been shown by a difference of termination, gender, or declension. Sometimes an Old English substantive and the verb derived from it have both survived, but, owing to the kind of sound-change which we have named 'divergent development,' the two have little or no resemblance in sound. Under these circumstances, the noun and the verb are no longer distinctly recognised as correlated in meaning, and the modern language has supplied the need for a closely-connected pair of words by turning the noun into a verb and *vice versa*. For example, the verb *bathe* is, as its spelling still shows, a derivative of *bath;* but in pronunciation the two have nothing in common but the initial *b*. Hence, we now speak of 'a *bathe*,' which does not mean quite the same as 'a *bath*'; and, on the other hand, the noun *bath* has given rise to a verb 'to *bath*,' which differs in meaning from 'to *bathe*.'

The following words of modern origin may serve to illustrate the freedom with which we can still form new derivatives by means of suffixes inherited from Old English: clever*ness*, clever*ly*, gentleman*ly*, rogu*ish*, think*er*, nois*y*, horseman*ship*. The English reader will be able at once to recollect many other words formed with each of these suffixes, and will perceive also that he might, without seeming at all eccentric in so doing, venture to use any one of them to form quite new words. Similarly, we can prefix the Old English negative particle *un-* to almost any descriptive adjective. There is another prefix *un-* (of different origin) which we can prefix quite freely to verbs to express a reversal of the action, as in *unfasten, uncover;* and the list of verbs formed with *be-* (like *befog, bemuddle*) is almost interminable.

There are one or two Old English suffixes for which the later language has discovered new uses. The ending *-isc* (now *-ish*) was in Old English chiefly used to form adjectives from names of places or peoples, as in *Englisc* English, *Lundenisc* Londonish. It was also appended in a few instances to common nouns to form adjectives of quality, as in *folcisc* popular (from *folc,* 'folk,' people), *cildisc* childish. The suffix *-ish* is still a living formative in both these uses. But about 1400 it began to be attached to names of colour, to form adjectives denoting a colour approaching that expressed by the simple word, as in *bluish, blackish*. On the analogy of the adjectives thus formed it afterwards became common to add *-ish* to any sort of descriptive adjective, in order to express a slight degree of the quality which they indicate. It was thenceforth possible, instead of saying 'somewhat good' or 'somewhat bad,' to express the idea by the single word *goodish* or *baddish*. To the characteristic English love of brevity this innovation was welcome; and in modern colloquial English we can append the suffix to most adjectives, of one or two syllables, denoting qualities that admit of degrees.

The ending *-ly,* representing the Old English *-líce,* forming adverbs of manner from adjectives, became in Middle English much more common, because the final -e, which in Old English was the ordinary adverbial suffix, ceased to be pronounced, so that the adjective and its related adverb became identical in form. Early in the sixteenth century, the need was felt for adverbs to indicate position in a numbered series; that is to say, for single words with such meanings as 'in the first, second, or third place.' The need was supplied by the addition of the adverbial ending -ly to the ordinal numeral, as in *firstly, secondly, thirdly, fourthly,* which were unknown to the older language.

Since the close of the Old English period, the vocabulary of our language has been enriched by a multitude of new derivatives formed with the prefixes and suffixes that already existed in Old English; and there can be no doubt that the formation of new words by this means will continue in the future. But the native machinery of derivation, though very little of it has become obsolete, has not been found sufficient for the necessities of the language, and has been largely supplemented by additions obtained from other languages. The adoption of foreign formative machinery has been rendered possible by the fact that many Latin and French primitive words have been taken into the English language along with their derivatives, formed with French or Latin suffixes. When such pairs of words as *derive* and *derivation, esteem* and *estimation, laud* and *laudation, condemn* and *condemnation*, had found their way into the English vocabulary, it was natural that the suffix -ation should be recognised by English speakers as an allowable means of making 'nouns of action' out of verbs. This particular suffix supplied a real want, because the only native means of forming nouns of action was the suffix -ing, which was not quite definite enough in meaning. It is true that this foreign suffix has not been very extensively attached to native words; as a rule, it has been felt to be more in accordance with fitness to adopt French or Latin nouns of action ready made. Still, such words as *botheration, starvation, fairation, flirtation, backwardation,* show that *-ation* has to some extent been regarded as an English formative. Another foreign suffix, *-ative,* though very common in words of Latin derivation, has been appended to a native verb only in one instance, viz. *talkative.* Such formations as *unwalkative* have been employed jocularly, but have never taken root in the language.

In some instances the attempt to naturalize a foreign suffix has failed because there was no real need to be supplied. Wyclif's *everlastingtee* (suggested by *eternitee* from *eterne*) did not find acceptance; the suffix *-tee* (now *-ty*) is confined to words either taken from French or Latin, or at least formed from French or Latin words. The native *-ness* answered all purposes, and the introduction of a foreign synonym was not required.

It was otherwise with many other French suffixes, such as *-age, -al* (as used in *withdrawal, upheaval, betrothal*), *-ment, -able,* which had nothing corresponding to them in English, and which have been used to form great numbers of words that the language could badly afford to do without. The endings *-ize, -ist, -ism, -ite,* originally Greek, have been very extensively used in the formation of English derivatives.

Old English, in comparison with most other Indo-Germanic languages, was remarkably poor in diminutive endings, and those which did exist were sparingly used. One of them was *-incel,* as in *tūnincel* a little 'town' or homestead; but this did not survive into Middle English. The ending *-ling* can hardly be said to have had a diminutive force in Old English, but it was frequently so used in Old Norse, as in *gæslingr,* which was adopted into English as *gosling* (dialectally *gesling*). The Norse suffix has in Modern English become quite common as a means of forming diminutive nouns. We have *kingling, princeling, squireling,* and many similar words. In the fourteenth century the Dutch or Flemish diminutive ending *-kin* (identical with the German *-chen*) came into English use, chiefly from nicknames like *Willekin,* little William, *Jankin,* little John. The fashion of forming such nicknames from Christian names became exceedingly popular, and has left abundant traces in modern surnames like Jenkins, Atkins, Dawkins, Wilkins. In imitation of these proper names, the suffix was afterwards attached to ordinary substantives, and in modern English we can, at least in jocular speech, add *-kin* to almost any noun to form a diminutive. Even more common than *-kin,* and more dignified in use, is *-let,* which we have adopted from French, and have appended to many native words, as in *cloudlet, streamlet, brooklet, leaflet, ringlet, booklet.*

There are two or three foreign prefixes that have been so completely taken into English that we use them almost or quite as freely as we do those of native origin. The most useful of these is the Latin *re-,* again. No dictionary will ever contain all the words formed with this prefix that have been used by English writers; the compounds of *re-* with verbs and nouns of action are as innumerable as those of *un-* with adjectives. In Middle English *again-* was often used as a prefix, but the words so formed have become obsolete: the English love of brevity has caused the native prefix to be supplanted by the foreigner. The Latin and French *dis-* comes next in frequency of use. Although Lydgate, writing about 1430, uses the word *distrust,* it was not until a hundred years later that it became a common practice to attach this prefix to native words. In 1659 a grammarian writes that *dis-*, like *un-* and *re*, "may be prefixed at pleasure." Perhaps this statement was even at that time somewhat exaggerated, and it would certainly be far from correct now. Of the multitude of words beginning with this prefix coined in the sixteenth and seventeenth centuries the greater part are obsolete (though many are still current, amongst them being such familiar words as *dislike, distaste, dispraise*), and since 1700 very few new ones have come into use. The prefix, however, is still felt to be quite English: no one would find any difficulty in understanding such a word as *dislove,* though it has perhaps never been used for centuries. Writers of the nineteenth century have used the verbs *disgod, dishero,* and the nouns *dishealth, discharity;* but formations of this kind have now an appearance of being affected. The French *en-* or *em-* has been used to form several English derivatives, as *endear, embody, embog, enliven, ensnare, entangle.* In recent times the Greek *anti-*, against, has become thoroughly naturalized. Words like *anti-slavery, anti-vaccinator, anti-income-tax, anti-corn-law, anti-radical,* are intelligible to every one, and their number is constantly increasing. Perhaps these formations should be placed rather under the head of combination than under that of derivation, though as the preposition *anti* has no separate existence in English this is a debatable question. There are other foreign elements which have in the same manner come into use as prefixes in the formation of English words, such as the Latin *pro* in *pro-Russian, pro-Boer; post* in *post-Norman, post-date; ante* in *antedate, anteroom* (imitating *ante-chamber,* which is French); *præ* in *pre-Roman, pre-Conquest; co-* in *co-mate; sub* in *sub-let; ex* in *ex-king; inter* in *interlock, interleave;*

non in *non-conductor, nonconformist, non-existence, non-natural.*

From these examples, to which many more might be added, it will be seen that the English language has not only very greatly enriched its vocabulary by direct borrowing from other tongues, but has also largely availed itself of foreign aid to increase its power of forming new words. There is very little in the borrowed machinery of suffixes and prefixes that can fairly be called superfluous. Almost without exception, it has been adopted, not out of foolish affection, but because it supplied the means of expressing necessary meanings with a degree either of precision or of brevity to which the native resources of the language were inadequate.

According to the definition which we gave of Derivation, 'the making of a new word out of an old one,' it includes two processes which have not hitherto been mentioned, but which have had a considerable share in the formation of the English vocabulary. These are *Back-formation* and *Shortening*.

Back-Formation.

There are many words in English which have a fallacious appearance of containing some well-known derivative suffix. It has not unfrequently happened that a word of this kind has been popularly supposed to imply the existence of a primary word from which it has been derived in the usual way. The result of this supposition is the unconscious creation of a new word, which is made out of the old one by depriving it of what is thought to be its suffix, or sometimes by the substitution of a different suffix. According to some eminent scholars, the verb *to beg* has been in this way formed from *beggar,* which is thought to be adopted from the old French *begar,* a member of the religious order called Beghards, who supported themselves, like the friars, by begging. This etymology is disputed; but there are many other instances of the process which are not open to question. The noun *butcher* is really from the French *boucher,* and the ending is not etymologically identical with the common English suffix of agent-nouns; but in many dialects people have come to use the verb *to butch,* and to speak of 'the butching business.' Other dialectal back-formations are *buttle,* to pour out liquor, from *butler,* and *cuttle,* to make knives, from *cutler.* The noun *pedlar* is older than the verb to *peddle* or the adjective *peddling,* and *broker* than the verb *to broke* (now obsolete) and the verbal noun *broking. Grovelling* was originally an adverb, meaning 'face downwards'; it was formed out of the old phrase *on grufe* (which had the same meaning) by adding the suffix *-ling,* which occurs in many other adverbs, now mostly obsolete, such as *backling,* backwards, *headling,* head-first. But *grovelling* was misunderstood as a present participle, and the verb *grovel* was formed from it. Similarly the verbs *sidle* and *darkle* have been formed out of the old adverbs *sideling* and *darkling.* Probably the modern verb *nestle* is not, as is commonly said, the same as the Old English *nestlian* to build a nest, but has been evolved from *nestling,* an inhabitant of a nest, used adjectively as in 'nestling brood.' Many of the words that have been formed by this process are so happily expressive that the misunderstanding that has given rise to them must be accounted a fortunate accident. It is to be hoped, however, that the adjective *swashbuckling* (formed from *swashbuckler,* literally one who 'swashes' or flourishes his buckler), which has been used by many recent writers, will not obtain general currency. Proper names ending in *-ing* have often given occasion to humourists to treat them as verbal substantives, and to evolve verbs from them. Some years ago there was much talk about the 'Banting method' of reducing corpulence, invented by a gentleman named Banting, and a verb *to bant* was for a time widely used. Still more recently, the uproarious rejoicings that hailed the news of the relief of the town of Mafeking, besieged by the Boers in 1900, suggested to some facetious journalist the formation of a verb *to maffick* (meaning to indulge in noisy demonstrations of patriotic joy), which is still common in newspapers, and has found a place in some dictionaries.

An excellent illustration of the working of this process is seen in the origin of the verb *edit*. The Latin *ēditor,* literally 'one who gives out,' from the verb *ēdere* to give out, was after the invention of printing often employed in a special sense as denoting the person who 'gives to the world' a book or other literary work of which he is not the author. In this sense it has passed into English and other modern languages. But under modern conditions there are two different classes of persons concerned in the production of a book, to either of whom the word might be applied in its literal meaning with equal propriety. The 'giver-out' of a book—for instance, of a classical text which has never before been printed—may mean what we now call the 'publisher,' the man who bears the expense of printing it, and makes the arrangements for its circulation among the public, or it may mean the scholar who puts the text into order for publication, and provides it with such illustrative matter as it is deemed to require. In early times these two functions were often united in the same person, but they are now ordinarily divided. Now while in French 'editor' (*éditeur*) has come to mean 'publisher,'

in English it has become restricted to the other of its possible applications. When we use it we no longer think of
its literal sense: the prominent function of an 'editor' is
not that of issuing a literary work to the public, but that
of bringing it into the form in which it is to appear.
Although *editor* is not a word of English formation, it has
an ending which coincides in form with that of English
agent-nouns, so that it has naturally suggested the coinage
of a verb 'to edit,' meaning 'to prepare for publication as
an editor does,' *i.e.* to put into such a form as is thought
suitable for the public to read. When we say, usually with
unfavourable meaning, that a war correspondent's tele-
grams have been 'edited,' we mean that they have undergone alterations or excisions in accordance with the press
censor's notion of the amount of information which ought
to be given to the public at home. Similarly, we may
say that the composition of an illiterate or foolish person
requires a great deal of 'editing' in order to be suitable
for publication. If instead of adopting the Latin word, we
had rendered it by some such equivalent as *outgiver* (corresponding to the German *Herausgeber,* which is used
quite in the English sense of *editor*), there would have been
no opportunity for the 'back-formation' of a verb with a
meaning so remote from the primary sense of the substantive.

Under the head of 'back-formation' we may not inap-
propriately refer to those instances in which an ending
common to a group of words has been treated as a separate
word, denoting the genus of which the things signified
by the various terms are species. The process is exemplified
in Bishop Warburton's definition "Orthodoxy is my doxy,
and heterodoxy is another man's doxy." As it happens,
doxy has not come into general use as a synonym for 'mode

of belief'; but we do speak, colloquially, of *isms* and *ologies;* and *'vert* (usually written with apostrophe) is, more or less jocularly, used to designate a person who, from opposite points of view, would be described as a '*con*vert' or as a '*per*vert.' The now common word *cycle,* meaning either a '*bi*cycle' or a '*tri*cycle,' is another example in point. Although it may suit the convenience of lexicographers to treat this word in the same article with the older word *cycle* (as in Tennyson's "a cycle of Cathay"), it is really an independent formation, which would have come into existence even if the other word of the same form had never been English.

Shortening.

The substitution, in hurried, careless, jocular or vulgar speech, of a part of a word for the whole, is common in most languages, and is especially congenial to the English fondness for brevity of utterance. It does not, by itself, constitute a mode of word-formation: the vulgar *taters* and *bacca* for *potatoes* and *tobacco,* cannot be called new words. any more than any other mispronunciations can be so called. But when, as very often happens, the original word and its shortened form come both to be generally used by the same speakers with different meanings, or even only with a difference in the implied tone of feeling, a real addition has been made to the vocabulary of the language, and the lexicographer is bound to recognise the shortened form as a distinct word. Shortening, in such cases, is in the strictest sense, a kind of derivation; and it is a process which has contributed not a little to increase the English store of words.

Even when the abbreviated form expresses precisely the same meaning as the original form, the two must often be reckoned as separate words, because the longer form is reserved for more dignified or more serious use. *Omnibus* and *bus* are synonymous in the sense that they denote the same objects; but they are not absolute synonyms, because the one is more familiar in tone than the other; the two are used on different occasions.* The same thing may be said of *photograph* and *photo*, or *bicycle* and *bike*, though here the abbreviated forms are not universally accepted by educated people as legitimate. Sometimes what was at first only a jocular abbreviation has ousted the longer form from general use, as in the case of *wig* for *periwig*, which was originally an altered pronunciation of *peruke*.

But very frequently a word which has been formed by shortening undergoes a sense-development of its own, in which the original word does not share. Even if anybody is pedantic enough to deny that *bus* is a distinct word from *omnibus*, he cannot refuse to admit that *cab* is a real word, though it was originally a shortened pronunciation of *cabriolet*. A cab and a cabriolet are not the same kind of vehicle at all. So too *Miss*, the title given to an unmarried woman, and *Mrs.* (pronounced *Missis*) are now quite different in meaning from each other, and from *mistress*, from which both are derived by shortening. There was a time when *gent* was used by educated people as a familiar abbreviation for *gentleman*, without any depreciatory implication. But in this use it was gradually discarded from the speech of the upper classes, and came to be a con-

* Moreover *bus*, and not *omnibus*, is now the international term used all over the world. *Bus* always denotes a vehicle except, of course, in such metaphorical expressions as *missing the bus* meaning 'losing an opportunity, failing in an undertaking'; whereas *omnibus* also functions as an adjective signifying 'serving every purpose in one' as in an *omnibus resolution*, or an *omnibus volume*, a book containing the whole work of one author.— Simeon Potter.

temptuous designation for the vulgar pretenders to gentility in whose vocabulary it still survived. *Cit* is a similar abbreviation for *citizen* or *city man,* though its use was contemptuous from the beginning.

Some words that originated as playful abbreviations of other words are now used without any consciousness of their origin. *Extra,* in such phrases as 'an extra allowance,' is not the Latin word, but an abbreviation of *extraordinary.* An *extra,* meaning an edition of a newspaper out of the usual course, was at one time called 'an *extraordinary.'* *Phiz* does not, to most people who use it, call up any recollection of *physiognomy;* and only students of etymology know that *chap* is a shortening of *chapman,* properly meaning 'trader.'

In the Middle English and early Modern English periods it was very common, in the hurry of pronunciation, to drop an initial vowel which immediately preceded the stressed syllable of a word. In this way many words beginning with a vowel came to have an alternative form from which the first syllable was omitted; and almost in every case in which both forms have survived a difference of meaning has been developed. *Assize* and *size* are so different in sense that no one could think of them as the same word, and yet the one is only a shortened pronunciation of the other. The standard magnitude of an article of commerce was settled by an 'assize' or sitting of some constituted authority. Hence the standard or authorized magnitude of anything was called its *assize* or *size,* and afterwards the latter form came to mean magnitude in general. *Tend,* as in the phrase 'to tend the sick,' was originally the same word as *attend;* but the two verbs are no longer synonymous. *Alone,* which stands for an earlier *all one,* was in the Elizabethan period shortened into *lone* when used as an adjective. The Middle-English phrase *on live,* equivalent to 'in life,' was commonly pronounced *alive,* and this, by shortening, afterwards yielded the adjective *live.* *Mend* was originally the same word as *amend.* The shorter form, as usual, serves for the trivial occasions of ordinary life, while the longer form is of more dignified application. We speak of *mending* a stocking, but of *amending* an Act of Parliament. Sometimes other prefixes than those consisting only of a vowel were dropped in the same way. The verb to *vie* is shortened from *envie*—not the same word as the modern *envy,* but adopted from the French *envier,* which comes from the Latin *invitare* to challenge; so that *vie* and *invite* are in ultimate etymology the same. *Fence* is *defence* without its prefix; and *fend,* from which *fender* is derived, is short for *defend.* Several words that originally began with *dis-* or *des-* now begin with *s.* *Stain* is a shorter form of *distain,* which is the Old French *desteindre,* to take out the dye of anything, from the prefix *des-, dis-,* and *teindre* to dye. *Despite,* from the Old French *despit,* the Latin *despectus,* a looking down, despising, has become *spite.* No word now sounds more thoroughly English than *sport,* which has, indeed, been adopted from English into foreign languages; yet it is a shortening of *disport,* which is a word of French origin. To 'disport oneself' is, literally interpreted, 'to carry oneself in a different direction' from that of one's ordinary business; and hence *disport* and *sport* came to mean amusement or pastime.

Besides the new words that owe their origin to shortening in pronunciation, there are others which have arisen out of abbreviations used in writing. Sometimes the mere initials of a phrase come to be treated as a word, the written letters being represented in pronunciation by their

names. Thus we speak of 'a question of £ s. d. (*el ess dee*)';
or, again, of 'an M.P. (*em pee*),' or 'a D.C.L. (*dee cee el*),'
meaning a person who is entitled to write those initials after
his name. Sometimes, again, a word or phrase as abbreviated in writing happens to yield a pronounceable sequence
of letters, and takes its place in the language as a word.
This occurs most frequently with Latin phrases. Many of
the shortened forms are vulgar or jocular, as *infra dig,
incog, nem. con.,* 'the *pros and cons.*' But *per cent, cent
per cent,* from the Latin (*centum*) *per centum,* are part
of the ordinary English vocabulary. The most curious
instance of the formation of a word by this process is *culprit.*
Its origin is to be found in the strange corrupt Norman
French once used in our courts of justice. When a prisoner
had pleaded 'not guilty,' the reply made on behalf of the
Crown was 'culpable; prest.' This meant '(he is) guilty,
(and we are) ready (to prove it).' In the reports of criminal
cases the phrase was commonly abbreviated *cul. prest,* and
afterwards corruptly *cul. prit.* Then in some way, not very
clearly understood, it seems to have come about that the
clerks of the Crown, modelling their procedure on the
pattern set in the written reports, fell into the practice of
using the syllables *cul prit* as an oral formula; and as this
formula was followed by the question, 'How will you be
tried?' addressed to the prisoner, it was popularly apprehended to mean 'guilty man.' The custom survived in the
courts down to the eighteenth century; but when *culprit*
became a current word with a new sense, it was probably
felt that there was an injustice in addressing a prisoner
by a term which presumed his guilt, and the use of the
formula was discontinued.

3. ROOT-CREATION.

Perhaps few, even among professed students of language, are aware how large a portion of the English vocabulary has, in the ordinary sense of the word, no etymology at all. We do not mean merely that there are many words the origin of which is and will always remain unknown because of the imperfection of our means of discovery. This is no doubt quite true. But there are also many words which were neither inherited from Old English, nor adopted from any foreign language, nor formed out of any older English or foreign words by any process of composition or derivation. It is to instances of this kind that the name of 'root-creation' may be fitly applied.

One of the principal forms of root-creation is that which is known by the name of Onomatopœia. The word is Greek, and literally means 'name-making.' It was used by the Greeks to express the fact (common in their own as in other languages) that a noise, or the object producing it, sometimes *makes its own name*: that is to say, is denoted by a word formed in imitation of the sound.

The number of 'echoic' words (as they have been called by Dr. Murray) which have arisen in Middle and Modern English is very considerable. We may mention as examples *bang, boo, boom, cackle, cheep, fizz, gibber, giggle, hiss, hum, mumble, pop, quack, rumble, simmer, sizzle, titter, twitter, whirr, whiz, whip-poor-will,* and the reduplicated words *bow-wow, ding-dong, flip-flop, hee-haw, ping-pong, pom-pom, rub-a-dub, tick-tack.*

It is possible that some of the words in the first part of this list may go back to Old English; words of this kind are much more common in speech than in literature, and we are certainly far from knowing the whole of the Old English vocabulary. However, even if they are much older than they can be proved to be, there is no doubt that they are imitative in origin.

The imitation of inarticulate by articulate sounds can never be accurate. Perhaps one or two birds *do* really 'make their names'; though even in the case of the cuckoo it is not quite certain that we actually hear the two consonants. But the cries of birds and animals, produced by organs having more or less similarity to our own, may be regarded as in some measure articulate. In general the rendering of noises into the sounds of human speech involves some play of fancy, like that which is exercised when we see faces in the fire, or landscapes in the clouds. The resemblance which an imitative word is felt to bear to the inarticulate noise which it names consists not so much in similarity of impression on the ear as in similarity of mental suggestion. For instance, it is not at all literally true that a gun, or a heavy body impinging on a door, 'says *bang.*' But the sequence of three sounds of which the word consists is of such a nature that it can easily be uttered with force, so as to suggest the startling effect of a sudden violent noise, while the final consonant admits of being prolonged to express the notion of a continued resonance. In this instance and in many others, the so-called 'imitative' word represents an inarticulate noise not so much by way of an echo as *symbolically*. That is to say, the elements composing the sound of the word combine to produce a mental effect which we recognise as analogous to that produced by the noise.

In much the same way, the sound of a word may suggest 'symbolically' a particular kind of movement or a particular shape of an object. We often feel that a word has a peculiar natural fitness for expressing its meaning, though it is not always possible to tell why we have this feeling, and the reasons, when we can trace them, are different in different cases. Sometimes the notion of natural fitness is an illusion, due to the fact that the word obscurely reminds us of the sound of several other words which happen to have meanings somewhat similar to that which it expresses. But quite often the sound of a word has a real intrinsic significance. For instance, a word with long vowels, which we naturally utter slowly, suggests the idea of slow movement. A repetition of the same consonant suggests a repetition of movement, slow if the vowels be long, and rapid if the vowels be short. The vowels that are produced by the passage of the breath through a narrow opening, such as *ee* or *ĭ,* are suited to convey the notion of something slender or slight, while a full vowel such as *oo* suggests a massive object. A syllable ending in a stopped consonant, especially an unvoiced one like *p, t, k,* preceded by a short vowel, affords a natural expression for the idea of some quick and abrupt action. Sequences of consonants which are harsh to the ear, or involve difficult muscular effort in utterance, are felt to be appropriate in words descriptive of harsh or violent movement. It would be possible to say a great deal more about the inherent symbolism of sounds; but it is not necessary here to pursue the subject in further detail. The point that needs to be remarked is that this phonetic symbolism (which probably had a large share in the primary origin of human language) has led to a very large amount of root-creation in Middle and Modern English. It is worthy of note that many of the words that have in this way been invented as instinctive descriptions of action or form occur in groups of two or three, in which the consonants are alike, while the vowel is varied to express differences of mental effect. Thus we have *bleb, blob, blub-cheeked,* all denoting something inflated. The initial *bl* was perhaps suggested by the verb *blow;* the pronunciation of the syllables involves an inflation of the cheeks which is symbolical of the notion common to the three words, and the different degrees of fullness in the vowels are obviously significant of differences of size in the object denoted. Other instances in which the notion expressed by the consonantal skeleton is modified by difference in the vowel are *jiggle, joggle; flip, flap, flop; chip, chap, chop; fimble, famble, fumble; flash, flush.*

Among the many words that owe their origin to a sense of the intrinsic expressiveness of particular combinations of sounds are *bob, brob, bunch, dab, dodder, fiddle-faddle, fidge, fidget, flabbergast, fudge, hug, hugger-mugger, hump, jog, see-saw, squander, squelch, throb, thump, thwack, twiddle, wobble.* Some of these, it is true, may in a certain sense be said to have an etymology; but their actual meaning is not due to the word, native or foreign, that may have suggested their formation in the first instance, but to the impression which is made by their mere sound.

Many excellent examples of intentional root-creation may be found among the invented words (not intended to be permanent additions to the language) in Lewis Carroll's *Alice in Wonderland, Through the Looking-glass,* and *The Hunting of the Snark.* These clever coinages derive their effect partly from their suggestion of obscure reminiscences of existing words, and partly from real phonetic expressiveness. Two of them, *galumphing* and the verb *to chortle,* have come into pretty general use, and have found their way into our dictionaries.

V

Changes of Meaning

In our discussion of the changes which the English language has undergone, we have hitherto spoken only of those which relate to its grammatical structure, and those which consist in the addition of new words to its vocabulary. We have yet to speak of another class of changes, not less important, though less conspicuous, than these: the changes, that is to say, which have taken place in the meaning of words.

The gradual change of signification in words is a universal feature of human language; and it is not difficult to see why it is so. Even the richest vocabulary must, in the nature of things, be inadequate to represent the inexhaustible variety of possible distinctions in thought. We can meet the continually occurring necessities of expression only by using words in temporary deviations from their ordinary senses. The dullest and most prosaic persons do this, of necessity and often unconsciously; those who have wit and imagination do it more freely and more effectively. Very often these novelties of meaning do not survive the temporary occasion which gave them birth; but when a new application of a word happens to supply a generally felt want it becomes a permanent part of the language, and may in its turn, by a repetition of the same process, give rise to other senses still more remote from the original meaning. Sometimes the primary sense remains in use along with the senses derived from it; sometimes it dies out, so that the word has exchanged its old meaning for a number of new ones.

It is owing to such progressive changes that so many of our words now bear two or more senses that are altogether dissimilar, and sometimes even contradictory. If, for instance, we turn to an ordinary dictionary for the senses of the adjective *fast*, we find that one of them is 'immovable,' and another is 'rapid in motion.' It would be obviously absurd to suppose that from the beginning one and the same word can have expressed two notions so entirely opposite. If we had no evidence to the contrary, we might guess that two originally distinct words had, in consequence of sound-change, come to be pronounced alike. There are many apparently similar cases in which this explanation would be the true one; but in the case of *fast* it is the meaning and not the sound that has altered, and the alteration is quite easy to account for. The primary sense of *fast* is 'firm, immovable.' But the notion of firmness, which appears in the expression 'to stand fast,' was developed, by an easy transition, into that of strength and unwavering persistence in movement. Hence it became possible to speak of 'running fast.' The adverb in this connexion originally meant 'without slackening'; but when it had acquired this meaning, it was natural that it should pass into the modern sense 'rapidly.' A later development of this sense is exemplified when we speak of 'living too fast.' 'A fast liver' and 'a loose liver' are expressions practically equivalent, although originally, and still in other connexions, the two adjectives are exactly opposite in sense.

The adjective *fine* affords another instance of a development that has issued in senses that appear mutually contradictory. It sometimes means 'slender' or 'small,' as in 'a fine needle,' 'fine grains,' and sometimes it means the very opposite. A character in a modern novel says: "He is not a *fine* child, for he is remarkably small; but he is a very pretty one." The original sense of the word is 'highly finished.' As the result of high finish is often to render the object worked upon delicate or slender, the adjective came in certain applications to denote these qualities, even when they are not the result of any process of elaboration. On the other hand, the notion of high finish naturally passed into that of beauty. Hence the word was used as a general expression of admiration; and in cases where large growth is a quality to be admired it practically assumes the sense of 'large.'

These curious phenomena might, perhaps, be paralleled in other languages; and even in English it is seldom that the development of senses has given rise to absolutely contradictory meanings for the same word. But the same causes which, as we have seen, have produced an exceptionally large amount of change in the grammar and in the vocabulary of English, have had a similar effect in the department of signification. Although we continue to use some thousands of words that already existed in Old English, there are comparatively few of them which now mean neither more or less than they did a thousand years ago. When we compare modern English with modern German, we find that very often the Germans continue to use a word in its oldest sense, while in our language its meaning is something strangely different. We will give a few examples.

The adjective *sad* had in Old English the sense of the corresponding German *satt,* satiated, full to repletion, having had all that one wants of anything. This continued to be the meaning of the word down to the fourteenth century. "Selden am I *sad* that semli for to se" (seldom do I have my fill of beholding that fair one), says a poet of the days of Edward II. But a person who has satisfied his desire for pleasure has lost his restlessness and excitability; he has become calm and serious, and more likely to attend steadily to the business of life. Hence in Chaucer's writings we find the word *sad* has acquired the senses of 'calm,' 'serious,' 'trustworthy.' In Shakspere it often means 'serious' as opposed to trifling or merry. "A jest with a sad brow," "in good sadness," are well-known examples of this use. But already in Shakspere there are many instances, such as "your sad heart tires in a mile-a," in which the sense of *sad* has been developed through its use as the opposite of 'merry'; and in the seventeenth century the word became restricted in its present meaning of 'mournful.' The midland and northern dialects of English show a curious side-development of the meaning of this word. By analogy with its use in describing persons who were serious and not easily moved, it has come to be applied to material substances in the sense of solid or compact. In Yorkshire 'sad bread' is bread that has not 'risen' properly, and is therefore not light or spongy, as good bread ought to be. The derived verb 'to *sad* down' means to press something down, so as to make it more compact; and hence the ironmonger's trade name for a smoothing-iron is *sad-iron.*

The original sense of *glad* has been preserved unaltered by the German equivalent *glatt,* which means 'smooth.' In Old English (as also in Old Norse) this meaning had already ceased to be current; but the word was still used for 'shining' or 'bright,' as applied, for instance, to gold, silver, jewels, and light. This was obviously quite a natural development from its primitive sense, for we make things shine by rubbing them smooth. It was equally natural that the sense of 'bright' should pass into that of 'cheerful' or 'joyous,' as it did already in Old English. The word has now quite lost its old physical applications, and, so far as plain prose is concerned, its figurative meaning has undergone some narrowing. Poets and rhetorical writers can still speak of 'a glad spirit,' 'a glad landscape'; but in ordinary talk we express this notion by other words, such as *joyous, joyful, cheerful, happy,* while *glad* is used only to characterize the state of feeling pleasure for some specified cause.

The German *Zaun* still retains its original sense of something that encloses, though the meaning is now confined to the special application 'hedge.' In Old English *tūn* (which is the older form of *Zaun*) meant a piece of ground enclosed by a fence, and specifically a farm with the buildings upon it. The Old English farm-houses, surrounded by the cottages of the labourers, developed gradually into villages, and some of these, in process of time, grew into still larger collections of habitations. Thus the word *tūn* (in modern English *town*) has gradually changed its meaning. From being applied to a single farm, it came to denote a collection of houses (the many place-names ending in *-ton* remain as evidence of this stage in its history), and finally (when it had been superseded in its humbler applications by the French word *village*) it survived only as the designation of an assemblage of dwellings larger and more important than a village. But, as readers of *Waverley* will remember, the Scottish dialect has retained *toun* in the

ancient sense as applied to a farm-house and its appurtenances.

Again, we still find in modern German the original
senses, or nearly so, of the verbs *write* and *read,* which in
English are used only in senses very remote from their
primitive use. *Write* is the same word as the German
reiszen, to tear. In the early Germanic tongue it meant
not only 'to tear,' but 'to scratch'; and in prehistoric Old
England it was specifically applied to the act of scratching
'runes' on a piece of wood or stone, and afterwards it was
extended to include the action—identical in purpose
though not in form—of marking a piece of parchment or
other material with signs that corresponded to spoken
words. This use of the word became so important that its
original sense was quite forgotten, and does not occur at
all in Old English literature. A word was needed to describe the action of interpreting the meaning of written
characters; and our ancestors supplied the want by using
the verb *read* (in Old English *rǣdan*), which meant, like
its modern German equivalent *rathen,* to guess a riddle.
The noun *riddle* (in Old English *rǣdels*) is a derivative
of this word. To the early English a piece of writing was,
we see, a mystery which only the wise could solve. The
new sense of the word did not, as in the case of *write,* at
once drive out the older one: indeed 'to read a riddle' still
occurs in literature, though it is no longer used in ordinary
speech. The German *rathen,* by the way, means not only
to guess, but to advise. In poetry, and in the Scottish dialect, *rede* still has this meaning, but we now regard it as
a different word from *read,* and distinguish the two by an
arbitrary variation in spelling.

The English *tide* is the same word as the German *Zeit,*
and in Old English it had the same meaning, namely

'time.'[1] But in Middle English its application was restricted, so that it meant chiefly the time of the periodical
rise or fall of the sea; and afterwards it was used to supply
the want of a name for these phenomena themselves. As
the older sense was sufficiently expressed by the synonym
time, the word could be set free for its new purpose.*

There are many other instances in which German has
retained the primary sense of a word, while English has
exchanged it for one that is widely different. And even
when the two languages agree in using a word in its original meaning, it will commonly be found that in English it has acquired a number of additional senses which in
German it has not. There is, it is true, no lack of examples
of an opposite kind,[2] indeed very few German words have
lasted a thousand years without gaining new meanings
or losing old ones. But it may perhaps be said that there
has been in English a far greater abundance than in German of those extreme changes by which a word comes to
express a variety of notions that seem to have nothing
whatever in common; and such changes have been hardly
less frequent in the part of the vocabulary adopted from
French and Latin than in that which is inherited from
Old English.

The changes of signification in English words would of
themselves furnish material for a large volume. In one
brief chapter it is impossible to treat the subject system-

---

[1] Preserved in *Christmastide, Shrovetide, Whitsuntide.*

[2] For instance, the English *clean* and *foul* have their original Germanic
senses; but in German *klein* has come to mean 'little,' and *faul* 'idle.'

* *Time and tide* was indeed an alliterative reduplication or tautology in
the proverb 'Time and tide wait for no man.' This proverb once had an
older form with threefold alliteration: 'Time and tide tarrieth no man'
where *no man* was the subject and therefore the verb was singular. —
Simeon Potter.

atically, even in outline. We shall therefore attempt nothing more than to call attention, in a somewhat desultory manner, to a few out of the many causes that have been operative in the development of new meanings, and in the disappearance of meanings that were formerly current. Additional illustrations of the principles set forth may be found on almost every page of the *Oxford English Dictionary,* a work which attempts to trace the history of every word in the language from its earliest appearance.

When we wish to express some notion for which we know no exact word, our easiest resource commonly is to use the word that stands for whatever other idea strikes us as most like that which we have in our mind. This process accounts for a very great proportion of the new meanings that words acquire. The nature of the likeness perceived or fancied differs in different cases. If it is a material thing that we wish to find a name for, the resemblance that helps us may be in form or appearance, as when we speak of the *eye* of a needle; or in some physical quality, as when the hard kernel of certain fruits is called a *stone;* or in relative position, as when the top and bottom of a page are called the *head* and *foot;* or in use or function, as when the index of a clock-dial is called a *hand,* because it serves to point to something. Sometimes two or more of these kinds of resemblance are combined: the *ear* of a pitcher is something like a human ear both in form and in position; in some English dialects the index of a clock is called not *hand* but *finger,* because it resembles a finger in form as well as function. Thousands of English substantives have in this way been provided with new senses. The word *chest* in Old English, and until the sixteenth century, meant merely a box; it has since become the name for that part of the body which contains the lungs and heart. A *needle,* as its etymology indicates (compare the German *nähen,* to sew), is primarily a tool for sewing; but we now apply the word to many things, such as the magnetized bar of a compass, which resembles a sewing needle in shape. The name of *horse* has been given to various mechanical contrivances which, like the animal, are used to carry or support something. The *key* with which we wind up a watch is so called, not because it resembles in shape or purpose the instrument with which we lock or unlock a door, but because in using it we turn it round as we turn a key in the lock. Nearly all the words denoting parts of the body have, as our dictionaries show, acquired a host of additional senses, because they have been applied to things that were thought to resemble in one way or other the organs or members to which the names originally belonged.

The foregoing illustrations have been confined to instances in which the name of one material thing has been transferred to another material thing that has been thought to resemble it. But the perception of resemblance, as a source of new signification of words, has been far more widely operative than these examples indicate. We are constantly finding that some immaterial object has a sort of likeness, not always clearly definable, to some other object, either material or immaterial, and so we use the name of the one to signify the other. Among qualities, conditions, and actions, we perceive similarities, either in themselves, or in their results, or in the feelings with which we regard them; and the words that express them, whether nouns, adjectives, or verbs, often acquire new meanings in consequence. When we speak of the *book* of nature, the *key* to a mystery, the *light* of knowledge;

when we describe a sound, a person's manner, or the condition of one's life, as *rough* or *smooth;* when we say that time *flies,* that anger *burns,* that commerce *flourishes:* we are using words in senses which we well know not to be their original senses, but which we feel to be justified by resemblances that are instinctively perceived, though many words might be needed to explain wherein they consist. In English, as in all other languages, this habit of metaphorical expression has played a large part in the development of the signification of words.

It is hardly necessary to dwell on the well-known fact that most of the words that are now used to describe mental states or qualities have obtained these meanings through metaphorical use, their earlier sense having been purely physical. This is, indeed, the ordinary course of development in all languages. But the history of the English language affords examples also of the contrary process. In Old English, the adjective *keen* could be used only of persons. It had the same sense as the German *kühn,* daring, bold, though it also had the meaning of 'wise' or 'clever.' In the thirteenth century the word that expressed the attribute of the warrior was applied to his sword. The physical sense, 'sharp, cutting,' rapidly became prominent, and the original meaning fell out of use. Although we can now speak of a *keen* thinker or fighter, these applications of the word are not inherited from Old English, but are metaphorical uses of the physical sense. The opposite of *keen,* as applied to a blade, is *dull;* and when we speak of 'a *dull* wit,' 'a *dull* brain,' we perhaps always have in our minds more or less the notion of a blunted edge. But in early Middle English *dull* could only be said of persons or their qualities. It is related to the Old English *dol,* foolish (corresponding etymologically to the German *toll,*

mad), and it expressed primarily want of intellect or ani-
mation. It was not until the fifteenth century that it
could be used of the edge of a knife; and the application
to colour or light is of equally late development.

The motive for using words in new senses is not always
that there is any difficulty in expressing the required meaning without such an expedient. It is often merely a desire
for freshness and vivacity of expression. Few people are
content always to say things in the most obvious way: an
accustomed word sometimes seems to lose its force through
familiarity, and the substitution of a picturesque or ludi-
crous metaphor enlivens the dullness of ordinary straightforward speech. This impulse accounts for the growth of
what we call slang. The substitution of *nut* for 'head' is
a typical instance of it. In some languages a large number
of words originally slang have displaced their more re-
spectable synonyms. For example, in vulgar Latin *testa*
(pot or shell) was used instead of *caput* (head), and this
is the reason why the Italian and French words for head
are *testa* and *tête*. Although the serious vocabulary of
English has not been so much influenced by slang as that
of some other tongues, there are some instances in which
the older words expressing certain meanings have been
superseded by jocular perversions of the use of other words.
In particular, there has been a curious tendency to grow
dissatisfied with the tameness of the verbs denoting violent
actions, such as throwing or dealing blows, and to substitute more emphatic synonyms. The Old English word for
'to throw' was *weorpan*, identical with the German *werfen*.
The Germans have been content to keep the old verb in
use; but in English it was superseded by *cast* (adopted
from Old Norse), and this in its turn by *throw* (corresponding to the German *drehen*), which properly meant to

twist or wrench. In many rustic dialects *throw* has gone the way of its earlier synonyms: the usual words in East Derbyshire, for instance, are *swat* and *hurl* (pronounced *oll*). The notion of striking was expressed by the verb now pronounced *slay*, which survives only in a narrowed and developed meaning, and even in this meaning is confined to literature. Here, again, German has kept the old word *(schlagen)*, while English has rejected it for more vigorous synonyms. In the King James Bible of 1611 the common verb in this sense is *smite*, which in Old English meant to smear or rub over. Its later use may be compared with the Elizabethan use of *anoint* for to cudgel, and perhaps with the modern slang *wipe* for a blow. But *smite* is now obsolete in ordinary language; the regular word is *strike*, the Old English sense of which was, like that of the equivalent German *streichen*, to stroke, wipe, rub gently. In colloquial use *strike* itself is to a great extent superseded by *hit*, which originally meant to meet with or light upon, and then 'not to miss' the mark aimed at. Although we still use the Old English *beat* with reference to the infliction of corporal chastisement, the more popular synonym is *thrash*, a lively metaphor taken from the language of the farm. In most provincial dialects there is an ample store of verbs for expressing this meaning, mostly figurative in their origin.

When the resemblances that have caused a word to acquire several new senses happen to be all of the same kind, the meaning of the word is often widened or generalized. That is to say, the word obtains a sense in which it is descriptive of all the various things to which it has been applied, and of all other things that share their common properties. This does not always happen. There is no general sense of *horse* in which the word is applicable both

to a racehorse and to a clothes-horse. In order that a
widening of sense should occur, it is necessary that the
common features of the several things denoted should be
such as to form an important part of the description of
each of them. A good instance of the process is afforded
by the word *pipe,* which originally meant a simple musi-
cal instrument, and afterwards (already in Old English)
was applied to other things resembling this in shape. It
thus became a general name for a hollow cylindrical body.
We are now apt to regard this as its proper meaning, and
to think that the shepherd's 'pipe' was so called because
of its tubular form. Sometimes the widening of the sense
of a word is progressive. *Box* in early use meant a small
receptacle (originally one made of boxwood, but this limitation had already been dropped in Old English), furnished with a lid, and intended to contain drugs,
ointments, jewels, or money. The sense grew gradually
wider, as the word was used to denote other things bearing
a close resemblance in form and use to those which were
previously designated by it; but down to the end of the
seventeenth century the word continued to be regarded
as appropriate only to objects of comparatively small size.
After 1700 this restriction disappeared, so that, *e.g.,* a chest
for holding clothes could be called a box. The notion
corresponding to the word is now so general that it is
equally applicable to what would formerly have been
called a box, and to what would formerly have been called
a chest. It is to be remarked that the word has many
modern applications, which, though connected with the
older senses by similarity, have not brought about any
generalization of sense. While we regard a pill-box, a
band-box, and a box for clothes as objects belonging to
one class, we have no notion of a wider class which com-

prehends these together with a box in a stable, a box in a theatre, a signalman's box, and a shooting-box.

Generalization of meaning takes place in verbs as well as in substantives, and some of the English examples are very remarkable. The verb *bend* is derived from the Germanic word which in English has the two forms *band* and *bond*. It meant originally to 'string' a bow, to strain it by pulling the string, in preparation for discharging the arrow. The result of this process being to give curvature to the wood, to 'bend a bow' was apprehended as meaning to curve or arch it by force; and then people spoke of 'bending' other things than bows, first in the sense of forcing them into an arched shape, and afterwards in the widened sense of bringing them by effort out of a straight form. The word has some other applications which do not historically belong to this generalized sense, though some of them are now thought of as derived from it. For instance, when we speak of 'bending one's powers to a task,' we are using what was originally a metaphor taken from the action of bending a bow. Again, the verb *carry* is an adoption of an Old French word which, in accordance with etymology, meant to convey something in a wheeled vehicle. In English it was applied to signify other modes of conveyance, perhaps at first by way of joke, as when nowadays people speak of 'carting' some object from one room to another. In the end, the verb became the most general expression for the act of removing a thing from one place to another by lifting it from the ground. In this sense it has to a great extent superseded the older verb to *bear*.

While generalization of meaning is one of the most common features in the history of words, there occur quite as many instances of the contrary process, whereby a word of wide meaning acquires a narrower sense, in which it is applicable only to *some* of the objects which it previously denoted. The reason why this process of *specialization,* as it is called, is so frequent is easy to explain. Even when we use a term in a very wide sense, we are seldom thinking of the whole class of things which it designates. The word *animal,* for instance, *may* indeed be used quite indeterminately, as when we are making a statement about all animals, or putting a supposed case in which it does not matter what species of animal is meant. But, far more frequently, we say 'this animal' when we know that we might as well say 'this horse' or 'this cow,' just as we often use the verb *go* when we might as well speak more definitely of *walking* or *riding.* If we have to mention some living creature of which we do not know the name, we can only call it an animal, though we know that the idea in our minds is more definite than that which this word implies. Now when a word of wide meaning happens to be very frequently applied to some one out of the many classes of objects which come under its general definition, the usual consequence is that the word, when used in particular circumstances, suggests the notion only of the limited class. Perhaps the general sense does not go out of use; but a new specific sense has been developed alongside of it.

The two contrary processes, of generalization and specialization, are very often illustrated in the history of one and the same word. We have seen how the word *pipe,* meaning originally a certain instrument of music, developed the general sense of 'a thing of tubular shape.' When the smoking of tobacco was introduced, people said that the smoke was drawn through a *pipe.* So far there was no specialization of meaning; and if the English had adopted some foreign name for the smoker's instrument there might have been no specialization, though we should still call the thing a 'pipe' when we were thinking particularly of its shape. Nor would the word have been specialized if it had always been convenient to speak of 'a tobacco-pipe' or 'a pipe for smoking'; but since in most cases the reference was clear enough without this troublesome precision, the simple word has acquired a specific sense, in which it is used quite without any mental reference to the wider meaning.

It is natural that the development of specific meanings, where the more general sense survives, should sometimes lead to inconvenient ambiguities, and in such cases a specialized use has often become obsolete, being superseded by the more frequent employment of some term that has no other than the restricted meaning. *To go,* which has properly about as wide a sense as any verb can possibly have, had in early English also a limited sense. Even so late as the end of the seventeenth century, Bunyan writes: "I am resolved to run when I can, to go when I cannot run, and to creep when I cannot go"; but this was already somewhat old-fashioned English. Earlier, such expressions as 'neither to ride nor go' were common. The German *gehen* still retains the narrower as well as the wider sense, but in modern English the narrower sense is expressed by *walk.*

Some general terms have acquired many different specific meanings, which do not cause confusion only because the circumstances in which they are used are different. The name of a material often becomes the name of several different articles made of the material. This does not always happen: there is no utensil commonly called a *gold,* a *silver,* or a *wood;* but a *glass* may mean either a drinking vessel, a mirror, a telescope, or a barometer, and there are

many other different applications of the word; an *iron* may
be an instrument for smoothing linen, a tool for branding,
a harpoon, or a kind of golf-club; a *copper* may be a copper
coin, a mug for ale, or a large caldron (and, by transference of application, now often one made of iron). It does
not appear that in such cases there has always been an
intermediate general sense 'thing made of the material,'
for many specific applications are missing which on that
supposition we should have expected to find. *Iron* does
not, like the synonyms in French and German, mean specifically a horseshoe, nor is *glass* ordinarily used for a glass
bottle. We may therefore regard most of the special applications above mentioned as having been produced by the
omission of the defining prefix in compounds: thus *glass*
in the senses above referred to is a shortening of *drinking-
glass, looking-glass, spy-glass,* and *weather-glass.*

The changes of meaning hitherto discussed consist for
the most part in the use of a word to stand for something
resembling that which it previously signified. Even the
processes of generalization and specialization may be said
to come under this head. But besides the perception of
resemblance, there are other causes that have had much
to do with the development of new senses of words. One
of these lies in the fact that most of the objects (whether
material or immaterial) which words denote are complex;
that is to say, they consist of several parts. When we think
of any complex thing, we seldom have in our consciousness
the idea of *all* its component parts; when we use its name,
we virtually mean, not the whole object, but only so much
of it as happens to be important for our mental point of
view at the moment. And sometimes, when we are thinking
of a definite individual thing, the possible mental points of
view are very numerous, so that there is a great variety of

partial conceptions any one of which is liable to be substituted for the total conception of the object. For instance, if a man says "that book," pointing to a volume lying on the table, there are at least half a dozen different things that he may mean. He may say "That book weighs half a pound"; and then the 'book' that he is thinking of consists of a number of sheets of paper and a leather or cloth cover. If he says "That book was unbound when I bought it," he is identifying the 'book' with the sheets of paper apart from the binding; but if he says "That book is the handsomest volume I have got," he may be referring to the binding only. If he says "I was just reading that book," the essential part of the 'book' is neither the paper nor the binding, but the black marks on the paper. Further, he may say "I had read that book before, but in another edition"; and then the 'book' is identified with a certain immaterial constituent of it, which may be defined as consisting of a particular series of words. And, lastly, if he says "I have read that book in several different languages," the 'book' means for him yet another immaterial part of the whole, viz. a certain product of mental labour, which retains its identity even when the series of words in which it is embodied is totally changed.

Now it would not be true to say that in these six examples of its use the word *book* has six different *senses,* in the lexicographer's acceptation of the term. The word denotes the same complex unity throughout, though the several statements made relate to different parts of this. But the illustration shows how the idea of any complex whole is liable on occasion to become virtually coincident with the idea of one or other of its parts; and in this characteristic of human thought we have the explanation of one of the processes by which new senses of words are developed. We continually find, in studying the history of a language, that a word which at first denoted some simple object has come to mean the compound object of which it is a part, and that a word which at first stood for a compound object has come to stand for one of the component portions. Very often, a word has first acquired an inclusive sense, in which it means the thing which it originally denoted together with other things commonly accompanying this; and afterwards it has been appropriated to the accompaniments themselves.

For example, the word *board,* in its specialized application to a table, has acquired two very divergent 'inclusive senses' and each of these has given rise to another sense from which the original notion has disappeared. On the one hand, *board* was used for the table with the food upon it; and hence it has come to denote food alone, as when we speak of 'paying for one's board.' On the other hand, the word was applied to a table together with. the persons who habitually sit around it to deliberate; a board of guardians of the poor, or a board of directors, is a number of persons jointly entrusted with certain deliberative functions. So too, in English as in many other languages, the word *house* has been taken to mean a building together with the persons inhabiting or occupying it, and hence it was successively used for a family consisting of parents and children, and for a wider unity of which a family is a part, consisting of persons connected by common descent, as when we speak of the houses of York and Lancaster. By a similar transference of meaning 'the House of Lords' and 'the House of Commons' are used for the members respectively of the upper and of the lower branch of the English legislature. The etymological sense of *world* is 'an age or generation of men.' Through the inclusive sense 'man and his dwelling-place,' the word has become capable of being applied to the earth itself, and hence by generalization of meaning, we can speak of 'uninhabited worlds' in space, or of the 'worlds' into which human souls pass after death.

The development of new senses through inclusive use takes place no less frequently with verbs than with substantives. In Old English the verb *wear (werian)* meant simply 'to be clothed with,' 'to have on.'[3] But the action of 'wearing' a garment, in this sense of the verb, will in time have the result of making it unfit for use. It will become threadbare, or it will be rubbed into holes. Hence, in Middle English, the verb obtained an inclusive sense, in which it denoted the action together with its consequence. Still later, it was often used with reference to the consequence only; and this meaning was afterwards generalized, so as to be applied to other objects than garments. In the King James Bible of 1611 we read, "The waters wear the stones"; and we can now speak of 'a face worn by trouble.' The twofold meaning of the word may sometimes give rise to ambiguity. 'A dress that is much worn' may mean either a style of dress that is fashionable, or an individual garment that is the worse for wear. When the verb is used intransitively, it may even have quite contradictory senses. We may say 'I want a cloth that will wear,' and 'I want a cloth that will not wear,' the two statements meaning exactly the same thing.

The original meaning of the verb *cry* is to utter a loud noise. But it was applied specially to noisy weeping; and in modern colloquial use the notion of making a noise may be dropped, so that we can say that a person is 'crying' who is shedding tears silently.

---

[3] It also had the sense 'to clothe.'

The history of the senses of the verb *drive* exhibits more than one instance of the process of which we are speaking. The primary sense of the word is exemplified when we speak of driving a flock of sheep; and it is with a very similar notion that a coachman is said to drive the horses. But the coachman's action includes not only the urging of the horses forward, but also the regulating and directing of the course of the vehicle drawn by them. The verb has come to be used for the whole action, of which the literal 'driving' is the least prominent part. When we say that a man *drives* a railway engine, we mean that he regulates the course of the engine, as the coachman does that of the carriage; but in the literal sense of the word he 'drives' nothing at all. It is a still further remove from the original meaning when the man in charge of a stationary engine is said to drive it. Again, the person who as coachman drives a carriage is travelling in it himself. The verb as applied to him has therefore an 'inclusive meaning'; and in modern use this may sometimes drop what was its primary element, so that *drive* comes to mean 'to travel in a carriage drawn by horses,' even if somebody else holds the reins. Here, as in a former instance, the development of meanings has resulted in ambiguity. 'He drives his own carriage' sometimes means 'he has a carriage of his own,' and sometimes 'he acts as his own coachman.'

In many cases a word has obtained a special shade of meaning through the accidental prominence of some particular association in which it frequently occurs. The verb *to harbour,* for instance, formerly meant generally 'to receive as a guest,' 'to give shelter to,' 'to entertain'; but, owing to its frequent occurrence in the proclamations which denounced penalties against the harbouring of criminals, it has come to be restricted to denote the sheltering of persons or things that ought not to be sheltered. In the figurative sense, we speak of harbouring evil thoughts, but not of harbouring good thoughts. Not long ago, an advertisement was quoted in the papers, in which a community of Italian monks appealed to English charity for subscriptions to their hospital on the ground that "they harbour all kinds of diseases." The expression was unfortunate, but in English of an earlier period it would have had no sinister meaning. The word *doctor*, literally 'teacher,' was given as a title to persons who had received from a University the attestation of their competence to teach some branch of learning; but, as the doctor of medicine was the kind of 'doctor' best known to people in general, the title was popularly regarded as belonging in an especial sense to the physician. Subsequently, in accordance with the common tendency to extend downwards the range of application of honorific titles, it came to be applied to any practitioner of the healing art, whether having a University degree or not.

It is similarly owing to the frequency of one particular association that *fellow*, which originally meant a business partner, and then generally a companion or comrade, has obtained the bad sense which it has in Pope's well-known line, "Worth makes the man, and want of it the fellow." In the fourteenth century, *fellow* was a condescending form of address (like the French *mon ami*) to a servant or other person of inferior station. We read in the poem of *William of Palerne* how "the Emperor called to him the cowherd, and *courteously* said, Now tell me, fellow, sawest thou ever the Emperor?" In the sixteenth century it was still customary to call a servant 'fellow'; and although this was no longer a mark of polite condescension, it did not imply any rudeness or bullying, as we are apt to imagine when we meet with it in the Elizabethan dramatists. But the frequency of this application rendered it unfitting to use the word vocatively to an equal in the sense of 'comrade.' To say 'fellow' to one not greatly inferior was naturally regarded as a gross insult, and hence it is that the word is now used to signify a person for whom one has no respect.

A very curious example of the way in which words originally of wide meaning have been restricted in their application may be seen in the history of the verb *to stink* and the related substantive *stench*. In Old English these words could just as appropriately be used to describe a delightful odour as a disagreeable one. It could be said that a rose *stinks* sweetly, or that a precious ointment was valued for its *stench*. When the five senses are enumerated by Old English writers, *stench* is the name for the sense of smell. But it seems to be a fact that unpleasant odours make a stronger impression, and are more frequently remarked upon, than those which are pleasing; and hence in Middle English these words came to be applied only to offensive sensations. In Old High German the verb *(stinkan)* had the same breadth of meaning as in Old English, but in modern German it means just the same as in modern English. It is noteworthy that while we have a special verb to express an unpleasant odour, English has no verb, like the German *duften,* to express the contrary meaning. It is true that English has adopted from Latin the adjective *fragrant* and the substantive *fragrance,* but these are rather literary than popular words. The substantive *scent* (derived from the French *sentir,* originally 'to feel or perceive,' but also used in the special sense 'to smell') is chiefly, but not exclusively, used in a favourable sense. The origin of the word *smell,* which has superseded *stink* and *stench* in their older neutral meaning, is obscure; it is found, both as noun and verb, as early as the twelfth century.

In some instances it has happened that one of the older words of the language has been almost entirely superseded by a synonym either of later growth or introduced from some foreign tongue, but has survived in one or two restricted applications. Thus the Latin *spirit* has taken the place of the native *ghost* in general use; but there are two noteworthy and very diverse applications in which the older word has remained current. One of these is the theological use. Formularies of religious instruction and ritual are never easily modified in diction, because the sentiment of reverence attaches itself to the traditional wording. The designation 'Holy Ghost' occurred in the baptismal formula and in the Creed, which from an early date were familiar in the vernacular to every Christian. Although it is now permissible to speak of the 'Holy Spirit,' the older expression still retains the special solemnity that belongs to the traditional terms of ritual; and at one time the substitution of the Latin synonym would probably have seemed almost irreverent. Yet it is only with the accompanying adjective that the word *Ghost* can be applied to the Divine Spirit. To say 'the Ghost of God,' or 'God's Ghost,' as was freely done in early English, would be utterly shocking, because every one now feels that the proper sense of *ghost* is 'the apparition of a dead person.' This use of the word was, for obvious reasons, the one that was most deeply rooted in the popular consciousness. The foreign synonym might displace the vernacular word so far as it represented ideas that were familiar only to cultivated people; in the sense in which it was used every day by the multitude it was not so easy to supersede it.

The history of the word *lord* is, on the whole, closely

parallel to that of *ghost*. It is a contracted pronunciation of the Old English *hláfweard*[4] or *hláford*, which literally translated is 'bread-keeper.' The word originally meant the head of a household in relation to the servants and dependents, who were called his 'bread-eaters';[5] and in Old English it had come to be the most general term for one who bears rule over others. In Middle English the French word *master* was introduced, and by degrees it took the place of *lord* in this wide sense. It is true that the Bible translators of 1611 still used *lord*, and not *master*, as the regular correlative to *servant*, and in poetry or elevated language the word can still have its original meaning; but so far as the diction of common life is concerned, that sense has been obsolete for many centuries. In fact *lord*, like *ghost*, is a native word that has been ousted from its place by a foreign synonym; but, like that word, it continues to be used in certain applications, one of them being religious. In the Old English service-books, *hláford* was adopted as the translation of the Latin *Dominus*, as applied to God and Christ,[6] and this use of the word had so prominent a place in the ordinary language of devotion that it could never be superseded. But besides its religious sense, *lord* had another specific application. A man of high rank was called 'my lord,' not only by his own 'bread-eaters,' but as a customary mark of respect by his inferiors in station generally. As the word *master* more and more

[4] This full form occurs only in one passage; in the usual form *hláford* the *w* was elided in haste of pronunciation, as in the modern *pennorth* for *pennyworth*.

[5] In Old English *hláf-ǽtan*: the word *hláf*, bread, is the same as the modern *loaf*.

[6] There was another word, *dryhten*, which was also used as a rendering of *Dominus* in this use. It survived into the fifteenth century as *Drightin*, but afterwards fell into disuse.

took the place of *lord* in its original use, *lord* became more and more definitely restricted to its use as a designation of elevated station, and was employed as a prefix to the names or territorial appellations of barons and nobles of higher grades. Hence, in modern times, when we hear of 'a lord,' unless there is something in the context to indicate some other meaning, we always understand the reference to be to one of those persons whose ordinary appellation has the prefix 'Lord' as indicating his rank. In Scotland, where the Old English *hlāford* came (in accordance with the phonetic laws of the northern dialect) to be pronounced not *lord* but *laird*, the word has retained a meaning nearer to its original sense, being applied to any owner of landed property. But as early as the fourteenth century, the English form *lord* was in Scotland adopted in the special meanings that had grown up in the southern kingdom —viz., as a title of the Deity, and as the designation for a nobleman.

Another Old English word that has undergone alteration of meaning through the introduction of a foreign synonym is *fēond*, in modern English *fiend*. This is a substantive formed from the present participle of the verb *fēon*, to hate. In Old English, and down to the middle of the fourteenth century, it was used, as the equivalent *Feind* still is in German, as the contrary of *friend*. In early Middle English the word *enemy* was adopted from French, and the native synonym gradually ceased to be used, except in the particular application which was common in sermons and religious discouse—viz., with reference to the unseen enemies of the souls of men. In the end, the original meaning of the word was quite forgotten, and it became simply equivalent to *devil*. A circumstance which seems somewhat curious is that, although the word owes its preservation to its having belonged at one time to the vocabulary of religious literature and speech, it has ceased to belong to this special vocabulary at all. It is not found in the King James Bible or in the Prayer-book, and is not at all frequent in sermons or other religious books. Its most prominent modern use is as a term of opprobrium for human beings whose exceeding wickedness suggests comparison with that of devils.

In the history of the synonymous adjectives *dizzy* and *giddy*, we have another instance in which a foreign word has usurped the ordinary sense of its native equivalents, but has allowed them to survive in one of their less frequent special applications. In Old English *dysig* (now *dizzy*) was the usual word for 'foolish'; it was also used substantively, so that *lā dysega* in the Gospels is the equivalent of "thou fool" in the King James version. *Gydig* (giddy) had the same sense. The etymology of these words, by the way, is extremely curious: the prehistoric meaning of both seems to have been 'possessed by a god.'[7] *Gydig* is a derivative of *god;* and *dysig* is from the Indo-Germanic root *dhwes-* represented in the Greek *theos* (from *dhwesos*) a god. However, in Old English the original meaning of these adjectives had already become obsolete, and they no longer denoted a 'divine madness,' but only commonplace want of sense. But early in the Middle English period the French word *fol* (a slang use of the Latin *follis*, a windbag) was introduced, and this word, in the modern form *fool*, still continues in use. It was originally used as an adjective as well as a substantive, and before the fourteenth century it had quite superseded both the native synonyms in their principal sense. But both *dysig* and

[7] As Greek scholars will perceive, this is the etymological sense of *enthusiastic*.

gydig had been occasionally used to describe the physical condition in which 'one's head swims'; and when the more prominent senses of the words had been driven out by their French synonym, this transferred application remained unaffected. In modern use *dizzy* and *giddy* are identical in their literal meaning; but we can now speak figuratively of 'giddy conduct,' so that the word has, in a roundabout way, undergone a sort of reversion to its Old English sense.

Again, the native English *stool,* like the equivalent German *Stuhl,* originally meant any kind of seat for one person, and might even be applied to a king's throne. It acquired its present restricted meaning because the French word *chair* had been adopted to denote the more luxurious articles of furniture which were in use among the Norman conquerors.

Once more, *deer* had in Old English the wide sense of the German *Thier;* but in Middle English this meaning was expressed by the French word *beast,* and afterwards the Latin *animal* passed from scientific into popular use. The native word continued to have its original sense down to the thirteenth century; about 1200 Ormin says "Lamb is soffte and stille deor," and still later we find the word applied to the lion. But even already in the thirteenth century it was becoming the specific name of the animal that was chiefly pursued in the chase. The older sense survived only in the expression 'small deer' for rats and mice, which in Shakspere's use is an echo from the old poem of *Sir Bevis.* If Caxton in 1481 once uses *deer* for 'beast,' that is only because he had lived so long at Bruges that he was more familiar with Flemish than with his native tongue.

A very large number of English words have undergone a

peculiar kind of change of meaning which consists in the addition of what has been called an 'emotional connotation' to their primary sense. That is to say, a word that originally served as a mere statement of fact comes to be used to express the speaker's feeling with regard to the fact. Note-worthy instances of this process are the adjectives *enormous, extraordinary,* and *extravagant.* In their etymological sense, these words merely express the fact that something passes the ordinary or prescribed limits; and in the English of former times they often occur in this matter-of-fact use. Thus 'an enormous appetite' formerly meant only what we should now call an abnormal appetite; 'an extraordinary occurrence' was one not in the ordinary course of things; 'extravagant behaviour' was behaviour which did not con-form to the accepted rules of propriety. But if we now employ these words, we mean to indicate not only that what is referred to is unusual or abnormal, but that it is so in such a degree as to excite our wonder, indignation, or contempt. In some cases, such as those just mentioned, the acquisition of an emotional sense has been helped by some-thing in the sound of the word; the long Latin derivatives, especially when they contain a syllable that admits readily of being either drawled out, or pronounced with excep-tional force, seem to be peculiarly liable to develop emo-tional senses. But the same thing has happened with many short words of native English origin. *Great* and *large,* for instance, mean to the understanding very much the same thing; but the former is an emotional word, and the latter is not. If I say 'I found a large table in my room,' I am simply stating a fact; but if I say 'I found a great table in my room,' I am expressing my surprise or annoyance. The emotional sense of the word has come into the language since the time when our villages received their names.

To our modern apprehension it seems comical that a small village should be called 'Great Tew,' because it is larger than the neighbouring 'Little Tew.' If we had the villages to name for the first time nowadays, we should probably say 'Greater' and 'Lesser'; the comparative of *great* does not share the emotional quality of the positive. In some of their applications, *little* and *small* are so absolutely synonymous that we can use them indiscriminately; but if any emotion is associated with the designation we must choose *little*. 'A small boy,' though a modernism, is now as good English as 'a little boy'; yet a foreigner who should exclaim compassionately 'Poor small boy!' would be very likely to excite laughter. We talk of 'a nice little house,' 'a charming little picture'; the substitution of *small* for *little* in these expressions would be grotesque.

Another word that has undergone this kind of change of meaning is *grievous,* which nowadays implies sympathy on the part of the person speaking, but which had certainly no such implication in the days when offenders were sentenced to be 'grievously whipped.'

When a word has acquired an emotional colouring foreign to its original use, it is necessary to provide a synonym that can be employed in a plain matter-of-fact way; and if no such synonym happens already to exist in the language, it is often obtained by altering the sense of some current word. The history of the words *large* and *small* is a good example of this. In Old French *large* originally meant liberal in giving, or prodigal in expenditure. This sense came into English: 'a large man' meant 'a generous man'; *fool-large* is an old word for 'foolishly generous' or 'extravagant.' The word developed in Old French the additional sense of 'ample in dimensions,' and afterwards came to mean 'broad' as opposed to long, a sense which remains

in modern French. In the English of the fourteenth century we find *large* used in these ways. When *great* had
acquired its emotional sense, and an unemotional synonym
was needed, the want was supplied by changing the meaning of *large*. The usual opposite of *large,* in the sense of
broad, was *small,* which originally meant narrow or slender,
as the German *schmal* still does. When *large* came to be
synonymous with *great,* the customary opposition of 'large
and small' still remained, so that *small* now means the same
as *little*.

Of the words used to designate unpleasant qualities, or
to express the feelings excited by them, many have come
to have a much stronger emotional meaning than that
which they originally had. In early English *foul* and its
derivative *filth* could be used (as *dirt* and *dirty* may now)
without indicating any strong feeling of repulsion. In fact
dirt was at one time a more emphatic word than *filth*.
The verb to *loathe* was originally not much stronger than
the modern *dislike*; the cognate adjective *loath* or *loth*
still expresses nothing more than mere reluctance. But
one of the most prominent applications of the verb was
to express the distaste for food felt by a sick person; and
as this is often attended with an actual sense of nausea,
the verb came to denote such an intense repugnance as
is felt for something physically revolting—something that
'turns one's stomach.' The derived adjective *loathsome*
has shared in this development of meaning; in early use
it was much less forcible than it is in modern English.
While *distaste, disrelish, dislike,* have not become more
emphatic than they were when first used, the originally
synonymous *disgust* is now far stronger in meaning. It
first appears in the French dictionary of Cotgrave (1611),
who renders *desaimer* by "to fall into dislike or disgust of."

We have already noted that *stink* and *stench* passed in Middle English from their original neutral sense to one expressive of unpleasant sensation; the intensity of meaning which they have acquired in modern use exemplifies the general tendency of which we are now speaking.

It is worth while to remark that in some instances words have undergone changes of meaning because in their literary use they have been popularly misunderstood. In the seventeenth century *ingenuity* had still its proper meaning of 'ingenuousness' or candour. Locke, for instance, could speak of an opponent's mode of argument as "more creditable to his acuteness than to his ingenuity," which to modern ears sounds like a distinction without a difference. But long before Locke's time the adjectives *ingenious* and *ingenuous* had become confused in popular use; even some very learned writers (or at least their printers for them) occasionally fell into the mistake of substituting the one for the other. Hence the noun *ingenuity* was often ignorantly or carelessly misused for 'ingeniousness' or 'ingeniosity,' and as these latter are both awkward words, while a noun answering to *ingenious* was more frequently wanted than one answering to *ingenuous,* the wrong sense ended by expelling the right one from the language. This is one of the many examples which show how powerless the regard for correctness becomes when it conflicts with the claims of convenience of expression. Another very similar instance is that of the word *preposterous,* which literally means only 'placed in reversed order,' 'put cart before the horse.' If a letter written to-day is delivered before one written yesterday, their arrival is, in the original sense of the adjective, 'preposterous.' But the word must often have been used in contexts in which its exact meaning was not apparent, and so unlearned people imagined that it meant something like 'outrageously absurd.' There is something in the sound of the word that fits it to receive an 'emotional connotation,' and it caught the popular fancy as an appropriate expression for contemptuous astonishment. The mistaken sense is now so firmly established that it would be mere pedantry to ignore it. *Emergency* is another word that is often used in a sense wrongly inferred from its contextual applications. Etymologically it means 'something that comes to the surface.' A case of emergency is a condition of things that comes up unexpectedly, so that it cannot be provided for by ordinary means. But when people speak of 'a case of *great* emergency,' it is evident that they apprehend the word to mean much the same thing as *urgency;* and probably the resemblance to the latter word has had some share in producing the distortion of meaning. In bad modern 'newspaper English' the verb *transpire* is used for 'to happen or take place,' and this sense has even found its way into recent dictionaries. Literally, to *transpire* is 'to breathe through'; and a circumstance may correctly and expressively be said 'to have transpired,' in the sense of having become known in spite of efforts made to keep it secret. It is through ignorant misapprehension of sentences in which the word was thus correctly used that it has come to bear a perverted meaning. As this blunder, unlike some others of the kind, does not supply any need of the language, it may be hoped that the misapplication of the word will not be permanent.

The current popular use of *premises* in the sense of 'a house with the outbuildings and the land belonging to it' is a striking example of the development of a new meaning through misunderstanding. In legal documents the word is used in its proper sense—'things *premised* or stated beforehand.' Just as the premises of an argument are the propositions laid down at starting, so in a lease or a deed the premises are the things specified at the beginning as the subject to which the following stipulations have reference. In the body of such a document, it is usual to employ the expression 'the premises' in order to avoid the inconvenience of repeatedly enumerating the various objects of which the occupation or ownership is transferred. As thus used, this expression is no more definite in meaning than 'the aforesaid' or 'the beforementioned'; but the thing to which it refers happens to be very frequently a house with its appurtenances, and hence it has been popularly apprehended as a name for this. On tavern signs we read that mine host is "licensed to sell ale and beer to be drunk on the premises"; in police reports a vagrant is said to be charged with "being on certain premises for an unlawful purpose." In the announcement "This house and premises to be sold," the word has undergone a further development of meaning, which the dictionaries have not yet recognised.

Sometimes, though not very often, a word has been so commonly employed in ironical language that its original meaning has been actually reversed. Although every Latin scholar knows that *egregious* is properly an epithet of praise, nobody would now feel complimented by being referred to as 'that egregious person.' Similarly, the adjective *sapient,* literally meaning 'wise,' can now hardly be used otherwise than in mockery. Here, however, the recollection of the proper sense of the word remains to give point to its contemptuous use. An instance in which a sense originally ironical has caused the favourable sense to be forgotten is afforded by *silly* (Old English *sælig*), which once meant 'blessed,' or 'happy,' like the equivalent Ger-

man *selig*. In Middle English it was often used satirically
in a tone of mock envy or admiration, and hence acquired
the disparaging sense which it now has.

It has been several times pointed out in this chapter
that the senses derived from a single primary notion may be
so diverse that it is only by a reference to the history of
their development that any connexion between them can
be discovered. This fact suggests the question what con-
stitutes the identity of a word. Regarded purely from the
point of view of modern English, *fast* meaning 'immovable'
and *fast* meaning 'rapid in motion' are quite as much distinct words as *light* in 'a light weight' and *light* in a 'a light
colour'; indeed there is rather more similarity of sense in
the latter pair than in the former. If, however, we look
at the matter from the historical point of view, we must
say that there is only one adjective *fast,* which has acquired
two meanings, but that the spelling *light* represents two
distinct adjectives, which once differed in form as well as
in meaning, but have come to be pronounced alike through
phonetic change. It is, in the abstract, quite as legitimate
to take one point of view as the other: to say that the adjective *fast* is always the same word, or to say that there
are two adjectives written and pronounced alike. But in
practice it is more convenient to decide the question of
identity by the test of origin than by that of signification,
because the most widely divergent senses of a word that is
historically one are usually connected by a chain of intermediate meanings.

This question, however, is of little importance except
to lexicographers. A matter of more general concern is
that development of meaning, while it has benefited the
English language in so many obvious ways, has unfortunately added very largely to the number of instances in

which the same group of sounds stands for radically different notions. From any point of view but that of the lover of puns, these 'homophones' are an unmixed nuisance. Our modern unphonetic spelling, bad as it is in most respects, has the merit of saving written English from a good many of the ambiguities of the spoken tongue. Most of the distinctions that exist in spelling and not in pronunciation are between words that are historically different, and when this is so the various spellings usually represent obsolete varieties of pronunciation. But in a few cases, the written language has been improved by the establishment of an arbitrary difference in spelling between what were originally senses of the same word. We have seen already that *read* and *rede* represent divergent uses of one and the same Old English verb; an old-fashioned spelling has been retained to denote the old-fashioned sense, while the ordinary sense is expressed by a spelling in accordance with modern analogies.

The verb *travail* or *travel* originally meant 'to labour,' and one of its specialized applications was in the sense of making a toilsome journey. This special use became generalized afresh in a new direction, so that the word now means simply to journey, however easily or pleasantly. But the Bible and other old books have preserved for us the memory of the original sense, so that it still occurs as an archaism; and as in the instance of *rede,* we render the old-fashioned meaning by an old-fashioned spelling. *Burrow* and *borough* are probably in origin the same word; their senses, different as they are, have been developed from the Old English sense 'stronghold.' In the sense of 'town,' which occurred very frequently in writing, an early spelling with *gh* became permanently fixed; in the sense 'hole made by an animal,' the word was seldom written, so that its spelling was uninfluenced by tradition, and represents a later pronunciation.[8]

Most people will be surprised to be told that there is no such word as *flour* in Dr. Johnson's Dictionary of 1755, and that he gives 'the edible part of corn, meal' as one of the senses of *flower*. Historically Dr. Johnson was quite right: the term 'flower of wheat,' which occurs about 1200, was only an instance of the still common figurative use of *flower* to denote 'the finest part' of anything. The original spelling of the word was *flour*, which continued to be occasionally used in all senses down to about 1700, though *flower*, introduced in the fifteenth century, was latterly the prevailing form. Early in the eighteenth century some writers began to avail themselves of the existence of the two spellings as a means of distinguishing the different meanings. The generally current form was naturally retained for the sense which was most common in literature, and with which it was therefore chiefly associated; the rarer spelling was left for the other use. Johnson was somewhat behind the times in not recognising a useful distinction which had been for some years established; but lexicography usually lags a little after usage. *Flower* and *flour* are now unquestionably two words, and in careful speech most people make a difference in pronunciation which is based on the artificial difference of spelling.

[8] Compare *thorough* and *furrow*.

VI

Some Makers of English

It is a truth often overlooked, but not unimportant, that every addition to the resources of a language must in the first instance have been due to an act (though not necessarily a voluntary or conscious act) of some one person. A complete history of the Making of English would therefore include the names of the Makers, and would tell us what particular circumstances suggested the introduction of each new word or grammatical form, and of each new sense or construction of a word.

Of course no such complete history could possibly be written. We shall never know anything about the myriads of obscure persons who have contributed to the development of the English tongue. And even if it were possible to discover the author of every new feature that has been introduced into the language since the earliest times, and the exact conditions under which it arose, the information would in all probability only very rarely have even the slightest interest or value.

But there are some Makers of English of whose personality we do know something: namely, the authors of literary works that are still in existence. The investigation of the extent of their influence on the language has a double interest. It not only gratifies our natural curiosity about the origin of the mechanism of English speech, but it also contributes in some small degree to our knowledge of the mental character of the writers, and thus enables us to attain a more complete understanding of their works.

Now there are two ways in which an author may contribute to the enrichment of the language in which he writes. He may do so *directly* by the introduction of new words or new applications of words, or *indirectly* by the effect of his popularity in giving to existing forms of expression a wider currency and a new value. If a popular writer happens to employ some comparatively rare word in a striking connexion, it will very likely come into the common vocabulary of the multitude, and then undergo a development in sense which would have been impossible if the word had continued to be confined to purely literary use. Moreover, when a passage of a poet or prose-writer becomes widely familiar as a quotation, the words of which it consists are apt to be used by later generations with a recollection of their particular context, and so to become either specialized or enriched in meaning.

In this chapter we shall give some samples of what certain literary Makers of English have done for the language. It is comparatively seldom that a word can be proved to have been used for the first time by a particular author; but it can often be shown that a writer has brought a word into general use, or that a current sense of a word is derived from a literary allusion. Of course it is not always the greatest writers whose works are in this indirect way most powerful in their effect on the language; literary excellence counts for less in this matter than popularity, and the ability to write passages that lend themselves to quotation.

It is important to point out that a great part of the work done by individual writers in the improvement of the language is of too subtle a nature to admit of being analysed or accurately estimated. A literary language has to meet requirements which do not arise in ordinary speech. The structure of sentences which suffices for the needs of oral intercourse is inadequate for written composition, where the thought to be expressed is continuous and complex, and where the aids to intelligibility furnished by intonation and gesture are wanting. As the art of literary composition advances, and the tasks to which it addresses itself become more ambitious, there is a constantly increasing need of devices for exhibiting more clearly the connexion of thought. The particles used for linking one sentence to another become more precise in their force, and new turns of expression, new syntactical constructions, alien to the language of conversation, are continually being introduced. Now every one of these improvements in a language is an invention of some one person; but it is obviously impossible, in most cases, to trace them to their authors. And hence it follows that, although we may be able to say what new words or meanings, or what phraseological combinations, are due to the influence of a particular writer, the effect of his works on the language may be far more important than it can be proved to be.

Among the works that have contributed to the formation of modern English an important place must be given to the translations of the Bible, from those of Tindale and Coverdale in the early sixteenth century to the King James version of 1611. The effort to find accurate expression for the thoughts of the sacred writers called forth abundance of ingenuity in the invention of new combinations of words; and the fact that the Bible has for centuries been the most widely read and most frequently quoted of books has made it the most fruitful source of allusive changes of meaning. The translations made before the invention of printing, especially that of Purvey in 1388, introduced many novelties of expression, but their circulation was too restricted for them to affect the general language as did the later versions. Besides, the translations from Tindale onward were not made, like those of earlier times, from the Vulgate, but from the Hebrew and Greek, or, at least, from Luther's German or from modern Latin versions directly based on the original texts. For rendering the expressions of the Latin Bible Wyclif and Purvey could avail themselves of the vocabulary that had been developed in English religious literature during the two centuries before they wrote. The recourse to the originals revealed new shades of meaning for which the traditional language of piety seemed inadequate, and the translators strove, often with felicitous success, to supply the new needs. To Coverdale we owe the beautiful combinations *lovingkindness* and *tender mercy;* Tindale gave us *long-suffering* and *peacemaker.* This last is identical in etymological meaning with the *pacificus* of the Vulgate; but the Latin word had become current in the sense of 'peaceable,' so that its literal meaning was obscured. Wyclif and Purvey render *Beati pacifici* by 'blessid be pesible men.' But when the sixteenth century translator found himself confronted with the Greek *eirēnopoioi,* the invention of an equivalent English compound was naturally suggested. It will be a surprise to most people to learn that such a familiar and, as we should think, indispensable word as *beautiful* is not known to have been used by any writer before Tindale. He certainly did not invent it, but there is no doubt that by introducing it into the People's Book he helped to bring it into general use. Another innovation of Tindale's has left a lasting mark on the language. By Wyclif and Purvey, the Latin word *presbyter,* designating an order of ministers in the Christian Church, had been rendered by its anglicized form *priest.* But in their translations *priest* stood also for another Latin word, *sacerdos,* which denoted the sacrificing ministers of the Old Testament. This was quite natural, because according to the view of the whole Christian world at the time, the priest or presbyter and the bishop were the successors in function of the sacrificing ministers of the Jews, and in Church Latin the word *sacerdos* was applied to both. When, however, the New Testament came to be translated into English from the Greek original, it was seen that the title *presbuteros* was the comparative of the adjective *presbus,* 'old.' Tindale retained *priest* as the translation of the Greek *hiereus* (the *sacerdos* of the Vulgate), but he thought that *presbuteros* ought to be translated by an English word of the same literal meaning. It cost him much thought to discover the right equivalent. In the first edition of his New Testament he used *senior,* a rendering which, in his controversy with Sir Thomas More, he admitted to be un-English and unsatisfactory. In his second edition he substituted *elder,* and in this he has been followed by all succeeding translators except those of the Rhemish (Roman Catholic) version. Thus Tindale's New Testament is the source of the ecclesiastical sense of *elder;* and the fact that in the English Bible *priest* never occurs as the designation of a Christian minister has had a remarkable effect on the popular acceptation of the word. Although the second order of the Anglican clergy are officially called 'priests,' it is only in certain northern districts that the people commonly apply the title to their parish clergyman. To the great majority of Englishmen the word suggests primarily either a Roman Catholic clergyman, or a minister of Jewish or heathen worship. Another noteworthy innovation of Tindale's is his clever rendering of *aischrokerdēs* by 'greedy of filthy lucre.' The substantive *lucre,* being known to most people chiefly as associated with the familiar and energetic adjective, has acquired a sinister sense which does not belong to it etymologically, and from which the corresponding adjective *lucrative* has remained free. Perhaps the most admirable product of Tindale's talent for word-making is *scapegoat,* which, though suggested by a misinterpretation of a Hebrew proper name, is a singularly felicitous expression of the intended meaning, and in figurative use has proved a valuable addition to the language.

The Bible translators after Tindale and Coverdale seem to have done but little in the invention of words and phrases that have become part of the language. But the indirect effect of the English Bible on the English vocabulary has been progressive down to recent times. Many words that were already somewhat old-fashioned in 1611, and would in the natural course of things soon have become obsolete, have been preserved from extinction because of their occurrence in familiar passages of Scripture, though they now belong only to elevated literary diction. Such are *apparel* and *raiment* for 'dress' or 'clothes'; *quick* for 'living'; *damsel* for 'young woman'; *travail* for 'labour.' The retention of *firmament* (the Vulgate *firmamentum*) in the first chapter of Genesis has given rise to the use of the word as a poetical synonym for 'sky.' While phrases used with conscious allusion to Scriptural incidents occur in all European languages, they are much more frequent in English than in the languages of Roman Catholic countries, where the Bible is directly familiar only to the

learned. We can speak, without fear of not being understood, of 'Gallio-like' behaviour, 'a perfect Babel' (not
always with capital B), 'a painted Jezebel,' 'a Naboth's
vineyard,' 'the Benjamin of the family,' 'the shibboleth of
a party,' 'Pharisee and publican,' 'the worship of mam-
mon,' 'a leviathan ship.' Our dictionaries explain various
senses of *Golgotha,* which are founded on playful references
to the rendering attached to the word in the English Bible,
'the place of a skull.' The appellation of 'the Prodigal
Son'[1] is current in allusive use elsewhere than in England,
but only in English is there a substantive *prodigal* in the
sense of one who has caused grief to his parents by aban-
doning his home.

Many Bible phrases, for the most part literal renderings
of Hebrew or Greek, have assumed the character of English
idioms, and are often used with little or no consciousness
of their origin. Such are 'to cast pearls before swine,' 'a
labour of love,' 'a howling wilderness,' 'the shadow of
death,' 'the eleventh hour,' 'to hope against hope' (a loose
version of Rom. iv. 18). Like most other books that have
been widely popular, the English Bible has sometimes given
rise to phrases and uses of words through misunderstanding. The current application of the phrase 'to see eye to
eye,' for 'to be of one mind,' has no warrant in the original
context. We sometimes meet with the expression 'line of
things' for a person's special department of activity or
study. The passage on which this is founded is: "And not

[1] This is not, strictly speaking, a Bible phrase, being derived from the
Latin of early commentators; but it occurs in the heading of Luke xv. in
the English Bible. The expression 'a good Samaritan,' which is current
also in French, is similarly of mediæval and not of Biblical origin. 'To kill
the fatted calf' is an allusion familiar throughout Europe; the wording
under which it has become proverbial in English was first employed by
Tindale.

to boast in another man's line of things made ready to our hand" (2 Cor. x. 16), where the intended meaning would have been clearer if commas had been inserted after the words 'boast' and 'line.' The common saying: 'He that runs may read' is a misquotation of "That he may run that readeth it" (Hab. ii. 2) which has a wholly different meaning. A striking instance of word-making through misunderstanding is *helpmeet*. In the Bible of 1611 the Hebrew words of Gen. ii. 18 were literally rendered "an help meet [*i.e.* fit, suitable] for him." Readers mistook the two words *help meet* for a compound; and so *help meet* became current as a synonym for one's 'partner in life.' People have been known to suppose that it meant "one who helps to 'make ends meet' "; but commonly when the word has been analysed at all, the second element has been imagined to be synonymous with *mate,* or perhaps an incorrect form of it. This notion suggested the formation of *helpmate,* which is a very good and correctly-made compound, though it did originate in a blunder.

It might well be expected that in any notice of the literary Makers of English a large place must be given to Chaucer. And indeed there can be no doubt that his writings had a powerful influence on the language; but it is singularly difficult to prove this by definite examples. It would be easy to give lists of words and expressions which are used by Chaucer, and, *so far as we know,* not by any earlier writer. We cannot doubt that a large proportion of these were really brought into literary use by him; a poet with so much of new thought to express, and so solicitous for fulness of expression, could not but avail himself of the resources which his knowledge of foreign tongues supplied for the enrichment of his native language; and he must often have found new and felicitous applications for words already current. Yet in individual instances we can seldom feel sure that in the use of this or that word he had not some English example before him. Further, when we see how much nearly all later English poets have learned from Chaucer, it seems certain that there must be a great deal of the modern poetic vocabulary which owes its currency to his example. But here, again, it is hard to find particular instances that are not open to doubt. Hardly any of his phrases—except "After the scole of Stratford-atte-Bowe"—can be said to have become part of the language in the sense in which this can be said of scores of phrases of the English Bible. For these reasons the share of Chaucer in the making of English must be passed over as not admitting of detailed illustration.

Spenser's influence on literary English is, if not really greater, at least more easy to trace than that of the poet whom he acknowledged as his master. While Chaucer was content to write in the language of his own time, and perhaps never consciously invented a new word or used an old one in a new meaning, Spenser deliberately framed for his own use an artificial dialect, the words and forms of which were partly drawn from the language of an older time and from provincial speech, and partly invented by himself. Ben Jonson's often quoted saying that "Spenser writ no language" is in a certain sense quite correct. Yet the choice of this peculiar diction was no mere affectation, nor was it due to any pedantic fondness for philological curiosities. Any one who justly appreciates Spenser's poetry must feel that his language, 'pseudo-archaic' as it may be called, was the only fitting vehicle for his tone of thought and feeling. It is true that by far the greater number of the words which he invented or revived have now become obsolete. But the literary vocabulary of the present day retains not a few traces of his influence. The familiar word *braggadocio* is an allusion to the proper name of the vain-glorious knight in the *Faerie Queene*. The phrase "squire of dames" comes from the same poem, though probably few of those who use it have any suspicion of its source. The adjective *blatant* appears first in Spenser, and it is not easy to guess its derivation; but it is now universally understood. Another word that seems to have been invented by Spenser is *elfin*. Dr. Murray has traced the singular history of *derring-do,* which was taken from Spenser by Sir Walter Scott, and through his use of it has become one of the favourite words of modern chivalric romance. It originated from a passage in which Chaucer says that Troilus was second to no man in "dorring do [*i.e.* in daring to do] that longeth to a knight." The passage was paraphrased by Lydgate in his Troy-book, and in the early editions of that work the word *dorring* was misprinted as *derrynge*. Not unnaturally, Spenser mistook *derrynge doe* for a sub-stantive (meaning, as his friend E.K. says in his 'gloss' to the *Shepherd's Calendar,* "manhood and chevalrie"), and employs it very frequently. The blunder has enriched the English language with a happily expressive word. Another of Spenser's debts to Lydgate is *gride,* which E.K. explains by "to pierce." Possibly it may have arisen from a scribal error for *girde,* to smite. In imitation of Spenser the word has been used by many subsequent poets, who have found something in its sound that seemed fitted to express the passage of a cutting weapon through flesh and bones. Shelley and Tennyson have adopted it to convey the notion of harsh or grating movement.

We now come to the greatest name in our literature.

Unrivalled in so many other ways, Shakspere has no equal with regard to the extent and profundity of his influence on the English language. The greatness of this influence does not consist in the number of new words which he added to the literary vocabulary, though we have already had something to say of the abundance and felicity of the compounds which he invented, but in the multitude of phrases derived from his writings which have entered into the texture of the diction of literature and daily conversation. We might call them "household words," without remembering that it is from himself that we have learned this expression. It would be possible to fill whole pages with the enumeration of the Shaksperian allusions which are in every-day use. 'Caviare to the general,' 'men in buckram,' 'coign of vantage,' 'a tower of strength,' 'full of sound and fury,' 'a Daniel come to judgment,' 'yeoman service,' 'the sere and yellow leaf,' 'hoist with his own petard,' 'to eat the leek,' 'curled darlings,' 'to the manner born,' 'moving accidents,' 'a Triton among the minnows,' 'one's pound of flesh,' 'to wear one's heart upon one's sleeve,' 'Sir Oracle,' 'to gild refined gold,' 'metal more attractive'—all these phrases, and very many others from the same source, may now fairly be regarded as idioms of the English language. If the reader thinks that this is saying too much, let him ask himself whether any man could be rightly acknowledged to be thoroughly master of modern literary English who was ignorant of the customary import and application of these expressions.

One Shaksperian phrase, "to out-Herod Herod," has not only become current in its original form, but has become the model after which a large number of other expressions have been framed. Among the many examples that might be quoted from eminent writers are "to out-Bentley Bent-

ley," "to out-Milton Milton," "to out-Darwin Darwin."
Shakspere seems in truth to have had a curious fondness
for the invention of compound verbs with *out-*, expressing
the notion of surpassing or exceeding. All the words of
this kind that exist in modern English appear to have been
either framed by him, or by later writers in imitation of
his example.

It would be easy to give a somewhat long list of words,
such as *control* (as a noun), *credent, dwindle, homekeep-
ing, illume, lonely, orb* (in the sense of 'globe'), which were
used by Shakspere, and have not yet been found in any
earlier writer. But such an enumeration would probably
give a greatly exaggerated impression of the extent of
Shakspere's contributions to the vocabulary of English.
The literature of his age has not been examined with sufficient minuteness to justify in any instance the assertion
that a new word was first brought into literary use by him.
Yet the fact that it is in his works that we so often find
the earliest known examples of words that are now current
is at any rate instructive, as showing the keenness of his
perception of the needs of the language.

When we turn from Shakspere to Milton, we find striking evidence of the truth of what we have already remarked,
that there is no constant relation between a writer's literary
greatness, or even the greatness of his fame, and the extent
of his influence on the language in which his works are
written. For, both in the estimation of the multitude and
in the judgment of critics, Milton's right to rank as second of English poets is hardly questioned; and yet, while
Shakspere has contributed innumerable phrases to the common treasury of English diction, the Miltonic expressions
that have really become part of the language are extremely

few. There are, of course, many passages of Milton that are very familiar as quotations; but there are not many of his combinations of words which we commonly use, as we do scores of those that are found in Shakspere or the Bible, without a distinct consciousness of their origin. There are some few from *Paradise Lost*: "to hide one's diminished head," "darkness visible," "the human face divine," "barbaric pearl and gold," "that bad eminence." From *Il Penseroso* we have "a dim religious light"; the companion poem has furnished one phrase, "the light fantastic toe," which few who use it ever think of associating with the grave Puritan poet. "Men of light and leading" is Burke's adaptation (brought into popular vogue by Disraeli) of an expression occurring in one of Milton's little-read controversial pamphlets. Perhaps, in estimating the debt which the English language owes to Milton, we ought to take into account the abundant material which his works afford for effective literary allusion. "Ithuriel's spear," "the last infirmity of noble minds," "writ large," the often misquoted "fresh woods and pastures new," are examples of the many echoes of Miltonic poetry which abound in subsequent literature. Of new words and senses of words brought into literary use by Milton it is not possible to find any considerable number. *Gloom,* in its modern sense of 'darkness,' may probably be his invention. Scottish writers had used the word for 'a scowl or frown,' and *gloomy* (derived perhaps from the verb to *gloom*) had been current since the end of the sixteenth century. Shakspere's "gloomy woods" may have suggested to Milton the formation of the substantive, which occurs nine times in his poems, but is otherwise unknown before the eighteenth century. *Pandemonium,* invented by Milton as the proper name of the capital city of Hell, the general place of assembly of the devils, is now freely used without any allusion to its literary source. That Milton had a genuine faculty for word-making, even though he chose to exercise it sparingly, is sufficiently proved by his invention of *anarch* as a designation for the personified Chaos. Three later poets, Pope, Byron, and Shelley, have availed themselves of this Miltonic word, and have used it with striking effect.

There are several words of Latin origin, e.g. *horrent, impassive, irresponsible,* which, so far as is known, occur first in Milton's works, and which it is possible that he may really have introduced. This, however, is a matter of little or no importance in relation to the estimation of the amount of Milton's share in the making of the language. In the middle of the seventeenth century words of this kind were, to repeat an expression which we have already used, *potentially* English; that is to say, the right of forming them at will, by anglicizing the form of Latin words or by attaching a Latin prefix or suffix to a word derived from that language, was in practice generally assumed and conceded. If Milton had not used these words, some other writer of the period would almost certainly have done so; and they may quite possibly have been employed by several writers, without any consciousness either of innovation or of following a precedent.

There are other writers, besides those we have mentioned, whose influence on the vocabulary and phraseology of literary English has been of great importance. We cannot, however, attempt to give here any account of their respective contributions, because the preliminary investigations on which such an account must be based have not yet been made. Among the authors who deserve special attention on account of the effect which their works have had on the language—either because of their boldness in the introduction of new words and senses of words, and the extent to which their innovations have found acceptance, or because their writings have afforded abundant material for literary allusion—may be mentioned Lydgate, Malory, and Caxton in the fifteenth century; Sir Thomas More and Lyly in the sixteenth century; Bacon, Philemon Holland, and Sir Thomas Browne in the seventeenth century; and Pope and Dr. Johnson in the eighteenth century. Coming down to later times, we may mention Sir Walter Scott, whose writings brought into general use many words which he found in older authors or in Scottish use, such as *raid, glamour, gramarye*. The works of Carlyle present an almost unexampled abundance of new compounds and derivatives, largely formed in imitation of German; and although comparatively few of those have won general acceptance, yet his influence has been effective in promoting a freer use of native English formatives than was tolerated in the early part of the nineteenth century. Some few words of his native Scottish dialect, also, such as *outcome,* have become familiar English from their occurrence in his writings.

The proper names of fiction and the drama have not unfrequently obtained a degree of currency in allusive use which entitles them to a place in the history of the English language. Bunyan's 'Vanity Fair' and 'The Slough of Despond,' and Defoe's 'Man Friday,' are virtually part of the English vocabulary, though they may not quite come within the province of the lexicographer. Swift's *Gulliver's Travels* has given us the words *Lilliputian, Brobdingnagian,* and *Yahoo,* the first of which, at any rate, is familiar to all educated English people. *Malapropism,* from the name of Mrs. Malaprop in Sheridan's play of *The Rivals,* is the recognised appellation for a species of blunder which is very commonly met with. The names of certain characters in Dickens's novels have given rise to derivatives in general use: every one knows what is meant when we speak of 'Pecksniffian morality,' or of taking a word 'in a Pickwickian sense'; and *gamp,* as a jocular word for 'umbrella,' may very likely survive when the allusion to Mrs. Gamp has ceased to be generally intelligible. The proverbial use of the names of personages in plays has often remained current long after the works from which they are taken have been forgotten. Few persons have read, or even heard of, Rowe's *Fair Penitent,* Mrs. Centlivre's *A Bold Stroke for a Wife,* or Morton's *Speed the Plough,* but everybody knows the expressions 'a gay Lothario' and 'the real Simon Pure,' and 'Mrs. Grundy' is constantly referred to as the personification of the tyranny of social opinion.

It is not unlikely that the future historian of the English language may find that its development in the nineteenth century has been less powerfully affected by the really great writers of the period than by authors of inferior rank, both British and American, who have had the knack of inventing new turns of expression which commended themselves to general imitation. There never was a time when a clever novelty in combination of words, or an ingenious perversion of the accepted meaning of a word, had so good a chance of becoming a permanent possession of the language, as now. In no former age was there such an abundance of writing of a designedly ephemeral character, intended merely for the amusement of an idle moment. The modern taste in style demands incessant variety of expression; the same thing must never, if it can be avoided, be denoted in consecutive sentences by the same word: and so those who are engaged in supplying the popular demand for 'reading matter' eagerly adopt from each other their new devices for escaping monotony of diction. When we consider that the literature which is for all time is read by comparatively few, while the literature which is for the passing moment is read by all, we may easily be tempted to think that the future of literary English is in the hands of writers of defective culture and little seriousness of purpose, and that the language must suffer grave injury in the loss of its laboriously won capacities for precision, and in the debasement of words of noble import by unworthy use. While these apprehensions are not wholly unfounded, there is much to be said on the other side. Even the much-decried 'newspaper English' has, in its better forms, some merits of its own. Writers whose work must be read rapidly if it is to be read at all have a strong motive for endeavouring not to be obscure; and the results of this endeavour may be seen in the recent development of many subtle contrivances of sentence-structure, serving to prevent the reader from feeling even a momentary hesitation in apprehending the intended construction.[2] We may rest assured that wherever worthy thought and feeling exist, they will somehow fashion for themselves a worthy medium of expression; and unless the English-speaking peoples have entered on a course of intellectual decline, there is no reason to fear that their language will on the whole suffer deterioration. In the daily-increasing multitude of new forms of expression, even though it may be largely due to

[2] One good instance of this is afforded by the frequency with which expressions like 'the fact that,' 'the circumstance that,' are now employed where formerly a clause would have stood alone as the subject of a sentence.

the unwholesome appetite for novelty, there must be not a little that will be found to answer to real needs, and will survive and be developed, while what is valueless will perish as it deserves. It is therefore perhaps not an unfounded hope that the future history of the language will be a history of progress, and that our posterity will speak a better English—better in its greater fitness for the uses for which language exists—than the English of to-day.

VII

English Present and Future

BY SIMEON POTTER

English is now the most widespread language in the world and second only to Mandarin Chinese, the *putong hua* or "common speech" of North China, in the number of people who speak it. After Chinese and English follow Hindi, Russian, Spanish, German, Japanese, French, Malay, Bengali, Arabic, Portuguese and Italian, in that order.

In the forms of its words and the structures of its sentences English is now remarkably stable but, because it is so widely diffused and because the external world is itself rapidly changing, English is inevitably prone to change. Other great international languages of the past—the Hellenistic Greek of the Mediterranean in the first years of our era, the Latin of the Roman Empire, and the French of the Crusades and medieval Europe—have changed with the years. Only in small enclosed communities like Iceland and Lithuania, segregated from surrounding peoples by sea or forest, mountain or marsh, do languages persist with little or no change over the passing centuries.

In present-day pronunciation we can certainly detect modifications affecting both vowels and diphthongs. For example, the middle and high-back vowels in words like *soft* (*coffee, off, often*) and *soon* (*boon, moon, room, spoon*) are being shortened. Many people still pronounce *often* and *orphan* as homophones, but most young Londoners now shorten the vowel of the former and—another important point to notice—they put in the *t* which has been silent for centuries. This is known technically as a *spelling pronunciation*. Few people, oddly enough, extend this sophisticated pronunciation to *soften* which they continue to articulate as before without enunciating the dental plosive after the labiodental fricative. In some ways this tendency to pronounce words according to their spellings is the most far-reaching of all because its effects are incessant and insidious. During the last century, since the Forster Education Act of 1870, the influence of spelling upon sounds has been continuous and cumulative. Unlike France and Turkey, the Netherlands and the Scandinavian countries, Britain has never altered its orthography by government action. Our spelling is basically the same as that of the fifteenth century East Midland scribes, which William Caxton (1422-1491) adopted when he set up his printing press at Westminster in 1476. Their way of writing was reasonably phonetic, though considerably less phonetic than that of Old English in the ninth century. Since Caxton's day pronunciation has changed in a hundred ways, but spelling has remained much the same. The gap between orthography and pronunciation has thus widened with every generation but, whenever people modify their pronunciation under the influence of spelling, they inevitably narrow the gap between the two. When they no longer say *sodger* as their ancestors did in the nineteenth century, but restore the *l* and say *soldier,* they bring sounds and spelling more closely together. By the way, do you pronounce the *l* in *falcon?*

British people are also modifying their pronunciation,

largely under transatlantic influence, when they restore fuller qualities to unstressed vowels. Doubtless this tendency will continue because it makes for greater clarity and distinctness both in television drama and in telephone communication. It will make English more like Spanish and Italian, and less like Russian.

Looking to the future, have we any hope that our spelling will be drastically reformed whether by government decree or by scholarly agreement? Our spelling is the most chaotic in the world. It is even worse than French. Whereas the orthography of that otherwise well-organized language is systematically unphonetic, English spelling is unsystematically unphonetic. Nevertheless, it has many advantages, and any attempt to undertake a wholesale reform on the basis of one symbol for one sound, as in Finnish, is rendered unfeasible by two plain realities. First, the pronunciation of English varies greatly throughout the world. Second, those varied pronunciations are ever changing. A reformed phonetic spelling would therefore satisfy only one small part of the English-speaking world today, and tomorrow it would satisfy no one.

Though wholesale reform is impracticable, minor improvements are both possible and highly desirable. We should be venturesome and enterprising even if, during an experimental period, we have to abandon the notion that correctness in spelling is one of the cardinal virtues. "Late, very late," said Pope, "correctness grew our care." The notion that a word has only one orthodox spelling is not older than the eighteenth century. After the experimental period, however, it is earnestly to be hoped that alternative spellings will be discarded and that trifling differences between British and American orthography will be leveled out by mutual agreement. Already much has been achieved by close coordination between the editors of *Webster's Third New International Dictionary* and the latest edition of the *Concise Oxford Dictionary* where first and second spellings of many words are given: for instance, *judgment* or *judgement* in *Webster*, but *judgement* or *judgment* in the *Concise Oxford*. On the other hand, whereas the *Concise Oxford* gives *realize, -ise, Webster* recognizes only the first, and so for all verbs in *-ize* (and nouns in *-ization*), showing directly or indirectly the Greek *-izein* and Latin *-izare*. Whereas *Webster* gives *plow* or *plough*, and *through* also *thru*, the *Concise Oxford* gives only *plough* and *through*. Since printing houses wield great power through their "style-directives," it would not be impossible for the leading British and American publishers to agree on one uniform spelling of every word now in use. At the same time it would be in the best interests of science and learning to preserve such valuable distinctions as *accessary* and *accessory, complement* and *compliment, discreet* and *discrete, premises* and *premisses, reflection* and *reflexion, set* and *sett, storey* and *story,* and many others.

Meantime other systems of recording English speech have been devised, of which the International Phonetic, the Initial Teaching, and the Shavian alphabets call for special mention. The International Phonetic Alphabet (IPA) was invented by French and British linguists in the late nineteenth century and it was used by Daniel Jones for the transcription of the London variety of Standard English in his *English Pronouncing Dictionary* of 1917 and all its subsequent revisions. It is indispensable for the teaching of English to foreigners. The Initial Teaching (Augmented Roman) Alphabet was devised by Sir James Pitman and others in 1964 for the teaching of reading to the schoolchildren of England in their early years. Of its forty-three so-called characters, eleven are digraphs. Its sole purpose is to supplement, and not supplant, the traditional alphabet, to which children revert at the age of seven. In this it differs radically from the Shavian alphabet of forty-eight letters, which was created by Kingsley Read in 1962 in accordance with instructions given in his will by George Bernard Shaw (1856–1950). In its general appearance this alphabet presents a compromise between Arabic and shorthand. Ten of its letters are designated as tall, ten as deep, twenty as short and eight as compound. The four most frequent words—*the, of, and, to*—are denoted by the single letters for *th, v, n* and *t*. Capitals are indicated by a preceding dot, but cardinal numerals are unchanged. This last feature is important since it reminds us that we already use two completely different forms for numerals: Roman and Arabic (strictly Indian). If we accept two sets of numerals, and if we are quite content to go on using them side by side, why not two alphabets? The advocates of the Shavian phonetic alphabet cherish the hope that it may win acceptance gradually, long supplementing the traditional alphabet before eventually superseding it.

As we turn our attention from the sounds and spelling of modern English to its word-forms, we note that inflections have changed remarkably little since Tudor times. The distinctive endings of the second and third persons singular present of verbs in *-est* and *-eth,* and of the second person singular past in *-st,* are now archaic. So, too, are *art* and *wert* in the forms of the substantive verb. The corresponding personal pronouns *thou* and *thee,* and the disjunctive pronoun and adjective *thine,* are also outmoded. After some three centuries of confusion between historically subjective *ye* and objective *you,* the former is now rarely heard in standard speech. Nevertheless the distinctions between *I* and *me, he* and *him, she* and *her, we* and *us, they* and *them* are well preserved, apart from a growing tendency to use the objective forms as emphatic subjective pronouns, and to say, for instance, *them and us* rather than *they and we* in alluding to classes or categories of people. *Us Londoners* sounds more intimate and friendly than *we Londoners.* In complementary position *It's me* and *That's him* are now generally accepted as emphatic variants of the more formal *It is I* and *That is he.* Otherwise the distinctions between subjective and objective forms are well maintained. All these pronominal forms are monosyllabic, they are in frequent use, and they can bear the main stress. They will therefore resist leveling processes indefinitely. Not so, however, the objective *whom.* As a relative, *who* is interchangeable with *that* and *which.* As an interrogative, *who* is the counterpart of *what.* All these three forms, *that, which* and *what,* have been uninflected for centuries. Is it surprising that inflected *whom* is unstable except when immediately following a preposition? "To whom did you give it?" but "Who did you give it to?" "That's the man to whom I gave it," but "That's the man I gave it to" with objective relative pronoun normally omitted.

One recent innovation is to be seen in the addition of the plural inflection *-s* to past participles, as in *retireds* "people who have retired from regular employment," or *unwanteds* "children born into the world unwanted by their parents." Traditionally these meanings would be expressed by a preceding definite article: *the retired* and *the unwanted.* So also *newlyweds* "couples recently married" and *coloreds* "non-white people having some proportion of Negro blood."

Another interesting tendency is the use of analytic forms with *more* and *most* to express the comparative and superlative degrees of adjectives instead of synthetic forms in *-er* and *-est*. This is one manifestation, however slight, of that drift toward the invariable word which has gone on in our language for thousands of years and which has proceeded to the very end in Chinese and Vietnamese. In this instance it is no more than a general drift. The old rules are valid. We still use *more* and *most* with adjectives of three syllables and more (*more beautiful, most beautiful*); *-er* and *-est* with those of one syllable (*brighter, brightest*); and either form with two-syllable adjectives (either *more lovely, most lovely,* or *lovelier, loveliest*). To-day, however, the analytic forms with the modifying adverbs *more* and *most* are gaining ground. Many people completely reject *commoner* and *pleasantest* in favor of *more common* and *most pleasant*. They say *more true* rather than *truer* and *most sure* rather than *surest*. They are even heard to say *more good* for *better*. Is this just a passing phase? Long ago George Gascoigne (in *Certayne Notes of Instruction,* 1575) advised aspiring versifiers to "thrust as few words of many syllables into your verse as may be: and hereunto I might allege many reasons. First, the most ancient English words are of one syllable, so that the more monosyllables that you use the truer Englishman you shall seem, and the less you shall smell of the inkhorn." At Britain's time of trial in the Second World War Sir Winston Churchill had "nothing to offer but *blood* and *toil* and *tears* and *sweat*." At pedestrian crossings the alternating signals are *wait* and *cross*. Old words like *nub* (the point or gist of an argument or problem) and *snag* (any unforeseen impediment) have been revived. Any

adept or proficient person in any capacity whatsoever becomes an *ace;* any purpose, design, object, aspiration or
intention, an *aim;* any interdict, prohibition, restraint or
denial, a *ban;* any offer, tender, endeavor or attempt, a *bid;*
any abridgment, abbreviation, shortening, curtailment or
reduction, a *cut;* any negotiation, agreement, transaction,
arrangement, concordate or adjustment, a *deal;* any organ-
ized effort or energetic action, a *drive;* any intuition, pre-
sentiment, sudden feeling, apprehension or foreboding, a
hunch; any undertaking, enterprise, achievement, perform-
ance, occupation, profession, employment, affair or task,
a *job;* any assembly, convention, congregation, conference,
conclave or synod, a *meet;* any petition, supplication, en-
treaty, appeal or request, a *plea;* any disparagement, slight-
ing remark, defamation, slander, libel, calumny or mis-
representation, a *smear;* any change, interchange, exchange,
reciprocation or alternation, a *switch;* any investigation,
inquisition, interrogation, examination, scrutiny, explora-
tion or inquiry, a *probe.* Such one-syllable words are much
in favor with commercial advertisers and with pressmen responsible for the framing of banner headlines. Too often,
alas, they will strain the meaning of their chosen monosyllable without scruple. Take, for instance, that last word
probe. This was primarily a surgical instrument for ex-
ploring the direction and depth of a wound—its only signification in Tudor times. Later, in the seventeenth century, the noun was used as a verb "to examine or explore
with a probe." Later still, in the nineteenth century, this
verb added a new sense to the noun so that it came to mean
both (a) the surgical instrument, and (b) the act of prob-
ing. It was, of course, this second use that opened the way
for all those present-day extensions of meaning which we
have broadly indicated.

Besides showing the increasing journalistic use of mono-syllables, this brief list also demonstrates no less clearly our superabundance of synonyms. Are they all necessary? The *Oxford English Dictionary* (corrected reissue of 1933) contains 414,825 words. *Webster's Third New International Dictionary* (1961) contains over 450,000 words. The wealth and diversity of our lexis or wordstore are un-equaled. Whereas, to take one very simple instance, French has *insomnie* and German *Schlaflosigkeit* for "the state of being unable to sleep," English has both *insomnia* and *sleeplessness*. Are they always interchangeable? No, they mean nearly, but not quite, the same thing. *Insomnia* signifies a pathological state, habitual inability to slide into slumber. *Sleeplessness* implies lack of sleep in general, and this may or may not be inveterate and lasting.

A person suffering from inability to sleep is now termed an *insomniac,* a derivative duly recorded in Webster but not to be found in any of the Oxford dictionaries. It may therefore serve as an illustration of that astounding revival of latent powers of composition and derivation which began in the United States about 1920 and which has since spread to other varieties of English. It marks indeed a movement from analysis to synthesis, a movement opposite to that leading to monosyllabism. In language, as in life, two antithetical processes may operate at the same time. This resuscitation of dormant powers of word-formation is truly remarkable. It is affecting the basic structure of our language. It is making English more like Greek and German, and less like French.

Today, for example, the classical particles *infra* and *ultra* are living prefixes, used and fully understood by people who have little or no knowledge of Latin. Such people have long been acquainted with expressions like *infra dig(nitatem)* and *ultra vires* but, with increasing knowledge of the light spectrum and spectral analysis, *infrared* and *ultraviolet* become everyday words. These epithets are applied to invisible rays *beneath* the limit of the red end of the spectrum and *beyond* the limit of the violet end. Both rays are frequently employed for various purposes in medicine and photography. So *infra-* and *ultra-* have now become living prefixes that may be added to any adjective. They have near-synonyms in *sub-* and *super-*, but certain fine distinctions must here be observed. Anthropoid apes (gibbons, chimpanzees, orangutans and gorillas) are *infrahuman:* men lacking culture or normal intelligence are *subhuman*. Sounds having a pitch too high to be detected by the human ear are *ultrasonic:* aircraft traveling faster than sound are *supersonic*. *Ultra-* also signifies "excessively or unreasonably extravagant" as in *ultraconservative, ultracosmopolitan* and *ultramodern*.

The prefix *mini-* is a startling innovation. Historically it is an abbreviation of Italian *miniatura,* an initial letter or a small picture in a medieval manuscript painted in *minium* or red lead. Because such pictures were inevitably small, people associated *miniature* with the root *min* in *minor* and *minimus*. In the early thirties of this century the Eavestaff Minipiano was registered as a trade name. In 1960 the British Motor Corporation produced its Mini Minor car and, since that date, *mini-* has proved a very prolific prefix indeed, producing *mini-bus, mini-car, mini-cam,* and *mini-budget,* not to mention *mini-skirt*.

Again, take the Greek prefix *para-* meaning "beside" as in *parallel* "beside one another," and *paraphrase* "beside telling, expression in other words." As a living prefix,

para- is also very prolific.[1] Since the mid-nineteenth century it has been employed by chemists to denote modifica-
cations of substances. For instance, the hypnotic drug
paraldehyde is a polymer of *aldehyde*. More recently, this
prefix has come to denote a branch of study that is beside or
beyond its acknowledged field, as, for instance, *parapsychol-
ogy,* an empirical science concerned with the psi phenomena
of extrasensory perception, including telepathy, clairvoy-
ance, psychokinesis and precognition. Philologists now talk
of *paralinguistics,* the study of marginal speech features like
pause, hesitancy, whisper and falsetto, that lie beyond the
domain of linguistics proper. The Greek prefixes *hypo-*
"under, below" and *hyper-* "over, above" are now used to
form hundreds of derivatives. So, too, are *anti-* "against,"
crypto- "secret, hidden," *neo-* "new, recast, recently invented," *pseudo-* "false, seemingly but not truly" and *proto-*
"first, original, primitive." Since English can draw freely
upon both Greek and Latin constituents, some fine distinctions can here be drawn. Compare, for example,
pseudo-archaic "artificially archaic in style"—like Spenser's
language (p. 158)—with *quasi-archaic* "apparently, but not
genuinely, archaic." Some Greek suffixes, it is true, are
limited to certain spheres: *-ectomy* to surgery, *-iatrics* to
medicine, *-phobia* to psychology. *Appendectomy* "excision
of the appendix" and *hysterectomy* "of the womb" are
twentieth century triumphs. *Pediatrics* and *geriatrics* are
impressive terms for the expert medical care of the young
and the aged. Have you any illogical or disabling fears?
Psychologists have amused themselves by giving Greek
labels to over one hundred of them. They include *acro-*

---

[1] Not to be confused with that other *para-* in *parachute, parapet* and
parasol from the imperative of the Italian verb *parare*—"to parry, ward
off, protect."

phobia "morbid dread of heights," *agoraphobia* "of public places," *ailurophobia* "of cats," *cynophobia* "of dogs," *entomophobia* "of insects," *photophobia* "of light," and *scotophobia* "of darkness," not to forget *triskaidekaphobia* "of the number thirteen."

Besides the classical prefixes *pseudo-* and *quasi-* just mentioned we may also use the synonymous native prefix *mock-*. Like German *schein-*, it has a forceful meaning, attributing downright shamness to the quality named. *Mock-archaic* is evaluative; it expresses stern disapproval and condemnation. The revival of classical affixes has certainly helped to give new life to native elements also. New adjectives have recently been created in *-y* and *-ish*, nouns in *-manship* and *-ness*, and adverbs in *-wise*. Derivative adjectives like *crafty, dewy, frosty, greedy, hungry, stony, thorny* and *wordy* are ancient. *Wordy* was *wordig* in Old English. Now numerous new derivatives in *-y* abound, some of them, it is true, still on the level of slang, but many already acceptable in careful speech. Many, but not all, are of transatlantic origin: some are British provincial. For *jumpy* the Oxford Dictionary gives no earlier record than *The Daily News* of 1869. Others like *cagy, chancy, choosy, edgy, preachy, snooty* and *tony* are recent. Derivative adjectives in *-ish* are also ancient (p. 95). This suffix was added regularly to national names as in *englisc* itself, which King Alfred, although he spoke West Saxon, invariably used to denote his own speech. Later this suffix *-ish* acquired a slightly pejorative sense as in *childish* as contrasted with *childlike*, and *monkish*, as contrasted with *monastic*. Its downtoning sense as in *stiffish* "somewhat stiff" and *whitish* "off-white" (French *blanchâtre*, German *weisslich*) is peculiar to English. Yet more remarkably it has in the twentieth century gained the meaning "round about, somewhere near," whether referring to the hours of the day in *elevenish* or to the years of a man's age in *forty-ish*. Old English *manscipe,* a rendering of the Latin *humanitas* and *manship,* "manliness, courage," long remained in use in the West Country. *Workmanship* is first recorded in the fourteenth century, *horsemanship* in the sixteenth, *craftsmanship* in the seventeenth, and *seamanship* in the eighteenth. It was largly due to the wide popularity of the mock-serious social studies of Stephen Potter (1900–   )—*Gamesmanship, Lifemanship* and *One-Upmanship*—that parasynthetic compounds in -*manship* became so prolific in the mid-twentieth century. Undoubtedly under Potter's influence Adlai Stevenson invented the sinister expression *brinkmanship* in 1956, a term in international diplomacy denoting the perilous art of advancing to the very brink of war without actually engaging in it. As for the abstract noun-forming suffix -*ness,* it has come to life again in such self-evident parasynthetic compounds as *divisiveness, forehandedness, outgoingness, togetherness, wide-awakeness,* and scores of others. A further outstanding example of the suddenly extended use of an ancient native suffix is -*wise.* In *clockwise, crosswise, likewise* and *otherwise* its use is old, but it is new in formations like *fashionwise* "in relation to present-day fashion," *moneywise* "financially," and *publicitywise* "in respect of publicity." This extended use arose in America where it may well have been influenced by the employment of the cognate -*weise* in the speech of German immigrants, as in *Beispielweise* "by way of example," a variation of *zum Beispiel* "for instance." Its adoption in Britain arises from a desire for compactness and a distaste for such cumbersome prepositional phrases as *with regard to* and *in connection with.*

New techniques need new terms. As the dauntless spirit of man takes him beyond "this goodly frame, the earth" into outer space, appropriate words are required to describe him in this unprecedented capacity. In 1961 the spaceman Yuri Gagarin became an *astronaut* or *cosmonaut* and these neo-Hellenic compounds became international overnight because the whole world knew at once of his exploit and shared in his triumph. No political or linguistic barriers circumscribe the new language of science. Thousands of new creations are labeled ISV (International Scientific Vocabulary), in *Webster's Third New International Dictionary,* actually the eighth in the series, which appeared in the very same year as Gagarin's space flight. They have been so designated by the etymologist Charles Sleeth because their precise origins are often unascertainable and because they are all "current in at least one language other than English." All the main arts and sciences —aeronautics, architecture, biology, building, chemistry, engineering, geography, geology, linguistics, medicine, metallurgy, physics, psychology, space travel— now have their specialized dictionaries which, compiled by experts, are highly competent and are constantly kept up to date.

As contrasted with word-formation, sentence-structures have remained fairly stable, but within inherited patterns word-classes continue to show functional shifts. Many parts of speech are made to serve other functions without danger of ambiguity because the syntactical frame into which they are fitted remains unimpaired and so makes everything clear:

John *pooh-poohed* the notion (interjection into verb) .
The water was *scalding* hot (present participle into intensive adverb) .

A lovelier *you* will leave our beauty parlor (pronoun into noun).

The director had a fit of the *blues* (adjective into noun).

Let us take a *break* for tea! (verb into noun).

Let *bygones* be *bygones* (past participles into nouns).

John knew all the *ins* and *outs* (adverbs into nouns).

Town life has its problems (noun into adjective).

The *then* Prime Minister acted on good advice (adverb into adjective).

In the third round the Mexican *floored* his opponent (noun into verb).

Wait for me on the *up* platform (adverb into adjective).

The Admiral *upped* (promoted) the young seaman on the spot (adverb into verb).

The cook likes to *brown* the potatoes (adjective into verb).

Not all these functional shifts are new. Some go back to the sixteenth century. But they are becoming more frequent and more daring in both speech and writing. They will doubtless continue to increase in the future because they are lively and effective. Some, it is true, are passing fashions: others are more or less facetious. Here, as always in communication, intelligibility is the salutary limiting factor. People want to be understood at once. An unusual shift, therefore, may not be immediately apprehended and it may take some time to be accepted by the community. For instance, the expression "For you this is a must" first appeared as an advertisement on a street poster about 1950. Later it was seen and heard on commercial television and, strongly stressed on *you* and *must,* this six-word ad made a hit. It appealed to viewers far more intimately and forcibly than more usual expressions like "You cannot go on living without this" or "For you this is an absolute necessity." The modal auxiliary *must* is here functioning as a noun. But no other auxiliary verb can yet be so shifted. No advertiser would be understood if he suddenly proclaimed "For you this is a *might*" (a remote possibility) or "For you this is an *ought*" (a moral obligation).

The most numerous shifts consist of direct interchanges between two basic word-classes, noun and verb. Such interchanges, as we have already seen are prominent features of North American English. Here we may note further some more recent uses of verbs like *construct* and *transform* as nouns even though the derivative nouns *construction* and *transformation* have long been available. At the same time we should be aware of subtle differentiations. The shorter forms are technical words denoting theoretical and mental processes: *construct* in logic and *transform* in mathematics. Yet more recently, both terms have come to be used in particular senses by linguists.

Attributive adjectives normally precede nouns in English, whereas modifying groups follow. We say "a mural painting" but "a painting on the wall," "a reference book" but "a book often referred to." Today, however, in their desire for greater brevity and compactness, people sometimes abandon this inherited principle and place an attributive phrase before, instead of after, the noun it modifies. They talk of "an often-referred-to book," "a once-in-a-lifetime experience," "a middle-of-the-road politician," "an off-the-record comment," "a round-the-clock discussion" and "a balance-of-payments deficit." In speech the exceptional functions of these phrases are made clear by intonation, and in writing by means of hyphenation.

Because phrasal verbs (p. 87) are made up of native components, they tend to be more vivid and vigorous than their classical synonyms. It is surely more forceful to speak of a *letup* than of a period of relaxation, and of a *setup* than of an organization, institution or arrangement. A *shake-up,* to be sure, implies some kind of very drastic re-organization. A *breakthrough* signifies a sudden advance (in scientific knowledge) in which some hitherto baffling problem is solved. A *frame-up* is an affair arranged with evil intent, especially one leading to the fixing of guilt or blame on an innocent person. A *lead-in* is an introduction or initiation of any kind. A *write-up* is a full description or report, usually one of praise. A *follow-up* is the next step after any action, especially a second advertising circular sent out after an earlier one. A *handout* is a piece of information given to the press for wide circulation. It may also take the form of a typescript summary distributed to students before a lecture. In the business world a *take-over* signifies the merging or amalgamation of two independent companies into one, and a *take-over bid* is an offer to make such a deal.

Side by side with this growth of phrasal verbs we also detect an increasing use of verbal phrases like *have a try* instead of plain *try* and *lay hold of* instead of plain *hold.* The first type consists of *have* + indefinite article + noun; the second consists of verb + noun + preposition. Both types express momentary aspect. To *have a try* or *a go* (in familiar speech *a bash, a crack* or *a shot*) means to try just once, to take a turn at doing a thing once. To *have a look* means to look once, to make one single act of looking. One can also *have a peep* (a furtive glance as through a chink or crevice), though not *have a see* since this verb does not normally express momentary aspect. But one can *have a bite, a taste, a drink, a smoke, a run, a ride, a swim,* or *a sleep.* The verbal phrase *catch sight of* means to see for the first time, and *set fire to* means to ignite once. Many verbal phrases, however, are merely stylistic variations without expression of momentary aspect, like *lay claim to* (demand as one's own), *find fault with* (criticize adversely), *set store by* (value highly) and *take care of* (watch over, protect).

This modern desire for brevity and compactness also gives rise to an augmented use of nominal phrases. If you compare the relationship in the following expressions between the attributive gerund and the noun it modifies you will see that in no two instances is it parallel; *baking powder* (powder for baking with, substitute for yeast), *cooking apple* (apple to be cooked, not eaten raw), *fishing village* (village whose inhabitants earn their living by fishing), *boiling point* (temperature at which a fluid is converted into a gaseous state), *laughing gas* (a gas, nitrous oxide, producing violent exhilaration when inhaled). The precise meaning of any nominal phrase is determined by its situational context. The reader of the newspaper headline —SMITH'S OLYMPIC GAMES HOPE—can only infer its exact meaning by implication, which may or may not be substantiated when he reads the article following: "Smith hopes that he will be selected to represent Britain in the forthcoming Olympic games." Too often such nominal phrases become unnecessarily overweighted. Instead of stating that "this is the verdict attained by the court of inquiry appointed to investigate the cause of a mysterious fire that broke out in a coach hired by holiday-makers," the six-word headline reads HOLIDAY COACH MYSTERY FIRE INQUIRY VERDICT.

Meantime the verb itself is undergoing significant changes. For one thing, its progressive forms are used more extensively than ever before. These forms indicate that an activity is regarded by the speaker as of limited duration. "John was going home when I met him" implies that

John happened to be returning from work and that during that particular period of time I encountered him. "John went home by car" states simply, without any specific reference to time or circumstance, that John drove home. Unfortunately, this distinction is no longer strictly maintained. Because the progressive form sounds more vivacious, people use it (are using it) undiscerningly. Is it only a passing fashion? No one would now ask with Polonius "What do you read, my lord?" (*Hamlet* II, ii). Everyone would say, "What are you reading?" No one would now cry with John Donne, "And therefore never send to know for whom the bell tolls. It tolls for thee." The injunction would more likely be, "Don't bother to inquire who that bell is tolling for. It is tolling for you." Whereas, until recently, verbs expressing mental states or attitudes like *believe, forget, hate, hope, imagine, know, love, see, smell, taste* and *understand* were never employed in their progressive forms, they may now be so used: "Poor Grandma is forgetting names nowadays." "My son is hoping to join us at Christmas." "You're surely imagining things." "We are all understanding the situation better now."

One important use of progressive forms is to indicate the immediate future: "I am flying to Boston." Yet more commonly this tense is expressed by *going* + infinitive: "I am going to fly to Boston." Old English possessed no separate form for the future. It had only two tense-forms: past and present-future. Unlike French, English has never developed verbal suffixes as it might have done if *(I) have to go* (now expressing, not future time, but compulsion or necessity) had become *(I) go-have-to* and if this composite form had later coalesced into one word. As we have already seen (p. 47), English has used the auxiliaries *will* and *shall* according to whether or not future events depend upon the volition of the speaker. When, in colloquial speech, both auxiliaries became reduced to [*l*], the distinction between them was blurred. Today "I'll be there" expresses both future time and mild intention. "I'm going to be there" means much the same, but with slightly greater emphasis on intention. Here *going* has lost its more restricted sense of *walking* (p. 128) and in the assertion "I am going to go" it serves as its own auxiliary. Only in the third person does it express a factual or colorless future: "It is going to rain."

The forms of verb-groups are changing more substantially than those of any other speech-categories. By means of participles and auxiliaries a highly intricate and subtle system of tenses and moods is being gradually evolved. Outwardly simple, this system is inwardly complex. At the same time it is both economic and effective. In this and in other ways the English language shows that it possesses within itself generative powers adequate to meet the many and varied demands made upon it by a technological civilization. From age to age the making of English continues without intermission. As a world language it is now subjected to many stresses and strains, but there are sure signs that the English of tomorrow will prove yet more efficient than that of today as a means of communication.

VIII

It Is Still Changing

BY BERGEN EVANS

If Bradley's book establishes anything it is that English has been continuously changing. And he feels that many of the changes, the results of millions of daily failures and successes in trying to convey meaning, have served to shape the language toward greater precision and more subtle perception, have served, that is, to make it an ever more perfect instrument of expression.

Many modern scholars would question this second supposition. They would doubt that any changes in any language are ever more than ceaseless adaptations to changing circumstances.

But no one would question the first of the two statements. English has changed and continues to change. It is, indeed, noticeably different today from what it was when Bradley first published.

Among the significant changes in English during the past sixty or seventy years may be listed the enormous expansion of its vocabulary, the proliferation of dialects in

some of the former British colonies,[1] accompanied, para-
doxically, by a decline, almost a disappearance, of dialects
and regional variations in Great Britain and the United
States, and the dominance, in standard English, of American English. Then there has been in speech, as in almost
every other department of life, a great increase in informality. And syntactical changes have also continued,
though at a slower rate.

Since thousands of coinages, borrowings and adaptations
are made every day, serve or fail their purpose, and disappear like bubbles in the surf, and since no dictionary
could begin to list them all, there are no figures on the
exact size of any language's vocabulary at any given time.
But some concept of the increase of words forced on us
within the past two or three generations by the explosive
enlargement of scientific and technical knowledge is suggested by the fact that Merriam-Webster's *Third New International Dictionary*, published in 1961, had to find space

---

[1] The reader who wishes an introduction to this fascinating subject cannot
be better advised than to consult "A Language in Common," a symposium
that makes up most of *The Times Literary Supplement* for August 10,
1962.

The layman will probably have a hard time believing that the following
introduction to *Macbeth* (in the pidgin of the Northern Territory of
Australia, as quoted in *The Times Literary Supplement*, May 6, 1965,
p. 350) can be taken seriously by anybody as a form of English:

> "Long time ago ole feller Donkey him bin big feller boss longa coun-
> try. Alright. By an' by another feller—him name ole Muckbet—bin
> hearem longa three feller debbil-debbil woman: them feller debbil-
> debbil woman bin tellem straight out—"You'll be big feller boss your-
> self soon." Alright. Him bin havem lubra, ole Lady Muckbet."

Yet any modern linguist would accept it as a dialect. And it is highly
likely that Aelfric (a part of one of whose sermons Bradley quotes in his
first chapter) would find it no more confusing or "corrupt" than standard
contemporary English.

for 100,000 words more than had been included in the *Second International* in 1934.

The vocabulary of physics, to choose a conspicuous example, is expanding with a violence almost commensurate with the new concepts and devices it has to describe. Aviation and aerospace have so far outstripped the lagging language that the United States Air Force has deemed it necessary to establish a department of lexicography to issue its own dictionary and word lists. Many large industries issue glossaries of special terms to their workers. Yet they are unable to keep pace with the increase of their own knowledge and techniques, so that the most striking feature, to the expert, of many of these lists is not their newness—though the ink is scarcely dry on their pages—but their obsolescence.

The layman may have the expansion brought home to him more strikingly by listing a few of the words out of the thousands that only yesterday he did not have. If a contemporary Rip Van Winkle had slept for forty years and awakened today, he would have to go back to school before he could read a daily paper or a magazine. For he would never have heard of such everyday things as atomic bombs, baby-sitters, coffee breaks, contact lenses or flying saucers. Nor of beatniks, eggheads, mambo, microfilm, nylons, parking meters, rock 'n' roll or splashdowns.

Many of the differences between American and British English go back to America's beginning when different groups of colonists brought different English dialects with them. Many others reflect the fact that from the time of their separation the two speeches began to diverge in independent developments.

Some of the words which the colonists brought with them, for example, and retained unchanged fell into disuse or changed their meanings in the motherland. Thus the American use of "I guess" to mean "I think" or "I suppose," though often derided by Englishmen who do not know their own literature, is as common in Chaucer as in Chicago. Shakespeare and Milton both used *homely* in the present American sense. When Shakespeare's doctor in *Macbeth* tells Macbeth that Lady Macbeth is "not so sick" as she is "troubled with thick-coming fancies," he is plainly using *sick* in the modern American, not the modern British, sense. Americans keep *pig* for young swine and *hog* for the mature animal, a useful distinction which the English have lost. Despite the uneasiness of some Americans and the contempt of many British, Americans preserve the old past participle *gotten* and the adverb *forth*. And until fairly recently one could hear, in rural areas, the old *clumb* (for *climbed*), *holp* (for *helped*) and *izzard* (for *z* or *zed*). In many parts of the American South *to carry* still has the old meaning of "to convey as a passenger in a wheeled vehicle." Many to whom these old forms are strange assume that they are innovations, "corruptions" of the language, and rail against them in indignant ignorance.

By the eighteenth century the colonies were beginning to be culturally self-sufficient. They had established their own speech, and the common people, at least, were content with their own way of talking. So that although most of the changes that had been made in pronunciation in England during the seventeenth century had been adopted here, most of the changes made in the eighteenth century were not. The most conspicuous of these was the broadening in British English of the *a* in such words as *glass, path* and *dance*. And it is interesting that this difference, which occurred just as the colonies had begun to resent their dependence on the mother country, became a shibboleth and is, even yet, the most resented by Americans of all the differences between the pronunciations of the two countries.

Not all peculiarities of our speech are leftovers, of course. Americans have been active in manufacturing or in borrowing from non-English sources whatever they needed. Strange flora and fauna were sometimes given names which in the homeland applied to different species (*corn* for maize, *robin* for a thrush, *buzzard* for a vulture). Or the Indian name, or what was thought to be the Indian name, was adopted (*opossum, raccoon*). In the Southwest, contact with Mexicans brought in a few Spanish words (*lariat, adobe, poncho, mesa, arroyo*) but only a few.

(Totally different is the very recent language problem presented by the influx of hundreds of thousands of Spanish-speaking people from Puerto Rico and Cuba, people who live in their own special communities, with their own teachers, newspapers and radio stations, and who show no inclination, as did earlier immigrants, to make English their everyday speech. So great are their numbers, however, and so secure is their political position that they may force America to become bilingual. And if they do, it will mark a division between American and British speech far surpassing anything previously known.)

Insofar as America has dialects or regional differences of speech, they consist of the peculiarities of vocabulary and pronunciation that one hears in New England, the region of New York City, the South, the hillbilly region—extending from the southern Appalachians west into the Ozarks, and the Pennsylvania Dutch country.

Of these, only the last-mentioned varies enough from Standard English to be regarded as a genuine dialect. It is used chiefly by the Mennonites of eastern Pennsylvania, especially those in the vicinity of Lancaster. And, actually, it isn't Dutch but an archaic form of German imported from the Palatinate fifty years before the American Revolution. In its pure form it was simply another language and can be regarded as a dialect only when so intermixed with English that English preponderates. Such it now largely is, but, despite efforts to save it, it is rapidly dying out.

As indeed are all marked differences in English on both sides of the Atlantic. Standardized public education, the popular press, movies, radio, TV, and the enormous increase in mobility in the population, especially during the two great world wars, have removed regional—and social —diversities with a speed unparalleled in the whole history of language. Since World War II the United States' strength in arms, her fabulous wealth, her technological skill, her literary and scientific achievements and, perhaps, her reluctance to hide any of these facts under a bushel, have spread her words and their ways, like a tide breaking through a dike, not only throughout British English but throughout French, German and even Japanese. In many lands thousands of patriotic and indignant linguistic "Dutch boys" have their fingers in thousands of holes. But their efforts are in vain: the inundation of American English must be accepted as one of the great facts of human speech in the mid-twentieth century.

The enlargement of our vocabulary, the increasing use of informality and the standardization of pronunciation are not the only changes taking place. There are also significant grammatical changes or the continuation of changes that have been operating for centuries.

Such changes, even when proceeding rapidly, take place only by generations, so that they usually pass unnoticed by all but grammarians. But even the layman can perceive them when he is told that something that seems "quite all right" to him was regarded as erroneous only a few years ago. (When, however, he is told that something that he considers wrong—such as the use of *like* as a conjunction or of *slow* as an adverb—has been accepted for centuries, he is still inclined to feel that it is wrong and that the language is improved by its finally being recognized as wrong.)

Take, for example, the increased use of the infinitive, one of the characteristics of modern American speech and writing. Ask any educated American to point out the grammatical error in "The government has a duty to protect the worker" or "We have a plan to keep the present tariff," and the chances are that he couldn't see anything wrong with either sentence. Yet in 1925 H. W. Fowler listed both of these sentences as ungrammatical. He felt that they should read "of protecting" and "of keeping." But the old form is now rapidly being superseded. Indeed, the infinitive has become so common in our speech that *to* is now often used by ellipsis to stand for any infinitive clause which has already been expressed—as "Are you going to tell him about it?" and its answer, "I intend to."

A further instance of change is the increase of what used to be called "empty" verbs. That is, where people used to say "Let's drink" or "Let's swim," there is now a tendency to say "Let's have a drink" or "Let's take a swim." Where people formerly said "It snowed heavily," we are inclined to say "There was a heavy snow." Our fathers *decided;* we, more cautious, *reach a decision*.

The reasons for such changes are obscure. Perhaps we are in the process of reducing our verbs to a few basic words of action—like those handy household tools where one handle serves for a blade, a screwdriver, a hammer, a corkscrew or any one of a dozen diverse implements that can be attached to it individually.

There are other changes: an increased use of the passive, for instance ("The house is being built" is now fully acceptable, though it was furiously opposed in the nineteenth century), and the increasing restriction of the possessive to nouns that name living things. That is, we speak of "the man's hand" but not of "the watch's hand." In the latter instance we would almost invariably say "the hand of the watch."

Bradley's prediction (pp. 37-38) that within a generation the subjunctive forms, except for *were,* would have ceased to exist has not been borne out. Indeed, the subjunctive formed by auxiliaries (*may, might, should, would, could, ought*) has been expanding, not withering away. But in regard to the old formal subjunctive, his assumption was sound. Such constructions as "Be he there, find him I will" would be understood today but would sound quaint.

Irregular forms have almost disappeared from English. But this does not mean that they will disappear entirely— certainly not in any foreseeable future. The few that remain, by their very remaining show that some strong force is preserving them. And this force is probably the frequency of their use, reinforced by the enormous conservatism of free public education—and its exaltation of "correctness."

However, irregular verbs are being regularized, especially in new applications. In America *crowed* has almost completely replaced *crew* as the past tense of *crow. Showed* has replaced *shown* (in England still *shewn*) as the past participle of *show. Knowed* is heard more often than *knew* among the uneducated but, perhaps for that very reason, does not seem likely to be accepted as standard. Remarkable changes are taking place, though, where a new application of a verb or noun makes a slight disassociation from the old word in the mind of the user. In applications to cattle, the plural of *beef,* for example, remains *beeves.* But in the slang meaning of "complaints," it is *beefs.* And anyone giving an order in a restaurant would certainly say "three roastbeefs," not "roastbeeves."

So also with verbs. *Baby-sitted* is heard more often than *baby-sat.* Fly balls are *flied* out to third. Disc jockeys say "I *spinned* that record only yesterday," and though this seems wrong somehow, at least to an older person, neither *span* nor *spun* seems right. We still say "She *wove* it herself," where the old idea of weaving is plain; but in the extension of the idea to the shifting movement of a car in traffic ("The truck weaved in and out as though the driver were drunk") *weaved* is certainly the preferred form in current usage. There is some hesitation between *dived* and *dove* in reference to someone's diving from a diving board, but an airplane or a market graph has always *nose-dived.*

The use of the colloquial in writing is increasing and the increase is accelerating. It is a part of the informality that changing social circumstances have forced—or encouraged—in many other departments of life. In dress and deportment, informality has gained acceptance, but in speech it is still met with a good deal of emotional opposition. From all sides we hear that the language (apparently assumed to have been "pure" until this moment, though the clamor against its "debasement" has been unceasing for the past three hundred years) is being "corrupted." Some alarmists go so far as to doubt that we will be able to communicate with each other in it within a few years unless something drastic is done at once.

Yet much of what is objected to has been in use for

centuries. From the uproar over "Winston Tastes Good *Like* a Cigarette Should," for example, one would have assumed that *like* had never been used as a conjunction before and that its being so used was expressly forbidden by Deuteronomy *and* Magna Charta. But Shakespeare so used it, and so did Dryden, Burns, Shelley, Masefield and Maugham and countless of their contemporaries. And so did and do millions of Americans. And all evidence shows that the construction is increasing in popularity and may very well—and very soon—render *as,* in this construction, obsolete.

Similarly, *none* has been regarded as a plural when its reference was plural from Elizabethan times on (see *Deuteronomy* 5:7). And double negatives have strengthened, not denied, negation as long as men have spoken English. Purists, from the clown in *Twelfth Night* to his modern counterparts, have insisted that two negatives make a positive, but no one in his right mind has any doubt what Chaucer meant when he said that his Knight "didn't never speak no villainy to no man." Or what any modern speaker of English means when he uses the same construction.

Then there is *who* at the beginning of a question, even when in the accusative. "Who did you give it to?" would have seemed as natural and "To whom did you give it?" as strainedly elegant a hundred or four hundred years ago as it does today. At least that's the way Marlowe said it ("Who have ye there, my Lordes?") and Addison ("Who should I see there but the most artful procuress?"). Noah Webster was emphatic on this point: " 'Whom did you speak to?' was never used in speaking, as I can find, and is hardly English at all."

The demand for "correctness" and "adherence to rules" of those who oppose the increased use of the colloquial will at best, if acceded to, sacrifice vigor to "propriety." At worst it is having an effect on the language by producing a new kind of bad grammar—the uncertainty and pretentiousness which substitutes *myself* for *me* ("He gave it to John and myself"), the sticking of *-ly* on the end of adverbs that don't need it ("She's doing finely!") and such vulgar elegancies as "Whom shall I say is calling?"

This new bad English might be called Intimidated English and the new semiliteracy which has to a large extent replaced the old illiteracy accepts its pronouncements as law. This would be all right if these "laws," like scientific "laws," were based on observation. But they are more like moral laws; they are promulgated on the assumption that there is some sanction for them beyond speech itself, some "higher" sanction in logic, decorum or social prestige.

One of the commonest effects of this is the belief that pronunciations that don't correspond to spelling are debased. "Slurred" is a common term for it. And those who let what their eyes have seen once overrule what their ears have heard a thousand times have poured scorn on such pronunciations as *mare* for *mayor*, *klōz* for *clothes* and *ak-choo-uhli* for *actually*.

Unfortunately for the scorners, however, these slurred forms happen to be the standard pronunciations, though they may not be for long. Increasingly, words are being pronounced as they are spelled. The "t" in *often* and the "l" in *almond, salmon* and *palm* are heard with increasing frequency. And even, to the dismay of the literate, the *c* in *indict*. Only the most aristocratic and the most *un*-aristocratic Americans now dare refer to *Saint Looey*.

If this brings spelling closer to pronunciation, it will be good. But if—as seems more likely—it brings pronunciation closer to spelling, it will be bad. Because English spelling, at the best, is only an approximation of past speech and much of it is simply wrong (like the *s* in *island,* the *h* in *ghost,* the *b* in *debt*). Then anything that establishes or helps to establish the primacy of written English over spoken English is bound to be confusing and to inhibit that spontaneity and unselfconscious concern with content rather than with form that is the foundation of effective expression.

It is increasingly plain that world unity requires a world language, at least a secondary tongue, in which international business can be conducted and international discussions carried on. And it is equally plain that this language will have to be one of the major languages now spoken, a language which hundreds of millions of people already speak and which, for various reasons—cultural, military, economic, it will be to the advantage of other millions to acquire.

Three languages meet these requirements: Chinese, English and Russian, with Spanish as a possible fourth. And of these English, at the moment, seems most likely to become the world's second language, the chief international means of communication. Its major advantage is that, due to historical accidents, it is the nearest thing to a world language we have. As the common speech of the two nations that for the past hundred and fifty years have possessed the greatest military and economic power in the world, it has been *the* language that enterprising men everywhere have striven to master. Hundreds of millions speak it as their native speech and perhaps a hundred million more use it as their second language. Many countries that appear on the map as unified wholes are, in reality, hopelessly divided linguistically. And in many of these it is not one of their own languages, but English, that is the lingua franca. In the riots in India, in 1965, over the establishment of Hindi as the official language of the country, riots that cost many lives and came close to being civil war, the placards and banners borne by the opposing groups were *in English*—because that was the only language that the educated on both sides could read. And in the anti-French demonstrations in French Somaliland, in 1967, the placards demanding that the French withdraw were not in French or Somali but, again, in English.

More printed matter and more broadcasted matter are in English than in any other language. In addition to the economic opportunities that a knowledge of the language offers, English also provides access to a great literature. And not least, it has a comparatively simple grammar, with every indication that it will be even more simple in the years to come.

But it has disadvantages as well. Though native speakers are happily unaware of the fact, it is hard to pronounce. The word *strength,* for example, which seems easy enough to us, might be appalling even to other Europeans—seven consonants and only one vowel! Then it is highly idiomatic. We may say "that man there," but "that there man" is regarded as illiterate. "Few men believe" and "a few men believe" have widely different significances. "Cleave" can mean to split or to stick together. "Either" can mean one or both of two. Many of our expressions have a meaning that can in no way be derived from their components. There is nothing, for example, in "good" or "by" to explain "good-by." And English is frequently ambiguous: "She takes a good picture," for instance, can mean that she is skillful in the art of taking pictures or it can mean that she appears well in photographs.

But the chief obstacle to the adoption of English as a

world language is probably its spelling, that fantastic lack of correspondence between our written symbols and our sounds which forces us to express forty or fifty sounds in approximately two thousand combinations of twenty-six letters. There is nothing whatever, for example, to tell the foreigner attempting to learn English that the present and past of *read* have different sounds, or that each of the three *e's* in *reenter* has a different pronunciation, or to guide him through the pronunciations of *through, cough, ought, slough* or *bough*.

Much hope for the use of English as the world's second language was aroused a generation ago by Basic English, a simplified form of the language worked out by C. K. Ogden and I. A. Richards. But though it retains much linguistic interest, it is no longer thought by any considerable number of people to be the inevitable solution. For although it would unquestionably make things easier for someone who knew no English but wished to speak it, it would be utterly unusable by any native speaker. That is, it would permit *them* to speak to *us* but would not permit *us* to speak to *them*. In contrast to pidgin—*their* way of bridging the gap—it would appeal only to those who would be most repelled by its condescension.

The unpleasant fact is that language follows the sword, imperialism and wealth. It was the legions, not Vergil, that made Latin a universal European language. French dominated commerce and diplomacy in the eighteenth century because France dominated Europe. And it was the British fleet, Manchester, Birmingham, and the thin red line that spread English in the nineteenth century. As it was Hollywood, Detroit, the American soldier and the Bomb that continued the spread in the twentieth.

Men who value peace and believe that freedom of discussion encourages peace sincerely hope that the world finds some language in which men of all races can speak to each other. Men who also value humanity and believe there is much to learn from the diverse experiences and diverse views of life rooted in diverse tongues, sincerely hope that there will never be only one language. It would be a catastrophic impoverishment.

Index